LOCKED IN A ROOM WITH OPEN DOORS

Other books by Ernest T. Campbell

Christian Manifesto
Where Cross the Crowded Ways

LOCKED IN A ROOM WITH OPEN DOORS

ERNEST T. CAMPBELL

WORD BOOKS,
Publisher
Waco, Texas

Grateful acknowledgment is made to the following for permission to include quotations from copyrighted selections in this book:

"Indian Children," from *For Days and Days* by Annette Wynne. Copyright 1919 by J. B. Lippincott Company. Copyright renewed 1947 by Annette Wynne. Reprinted by permission of J. B. Lippincott Company.

"For the Time Being: A Christmas Oratorio," copyright 1944 and renewed 1972 by W. H. Auden. Reprinted from *Collected Longer Poems*, by W. H. Auden, by permission of Random House, Inc.

The Everlasting Mercy by John Masefield. Reprinted with permission of Macmillan Publishing Co., Inc. Copyright 1912 by Macmillan Publishing Co., Inc., renewed 1940 by John Masefield.

Scripture quotations, unless otherwise noted, are from the Revised Standard Version of the Bible, copyright 1946 (renewed 1973), 1956 and © 1971 by the Division of Christian Education of the National Council of the Churches of Christ in the USA, and are used by permission.

Scripture quotations marked NEB are from *The New English Bible* © The Delegates of the Oxford University Press and the Syndics of the Cambridge University Press, 1961, 1970, and are used by permission.

The author's royalties go in their entirety
to the NAACP Legal Defense Fund, to whose work
and vision this volume is gratefully dedicated

Contents

Author's Preface

Preaching of late has experienced a depressed market. In an era in which words fall on the ears of man with torrential steadiness and force it is understandable that all human speech should be severely discounted.

Moreover, recent decades have put a premium on action, not speech. What are words against the unconscionably long list of social, political, and economic inequities that fairly scream for redress? Small wonder that many ministers adjudged it a wiser expenditure of time to organize a march than a sermon.

Then too, the entire enterprise of faith has of late been under heavy fire. Applied science seemingly achieves more than applied prayer in today's kind of world. The good life is increasingly defined in terms of material well-being. While Jesus still manages to keep his hold on humankind, moderns do not blush to call the church an anachronism or to pro-

9

nounce God dead. In such a context preaching is easily dismissed as a harmless exercise performed by those who can do no other because they are vocationally trapped.

At this writing there are signs that preaching is coming back. Seminaries across the land report a new interest in preaching. Preaching as a unique phenomenon in the Hebrew-Christian tradition is in many quarters being enthusiastically rediscovered. This is markedly true in the Roman Catholic Church.

The inadequacies of material abundance are showing through. Goods are no substitute for purpose or belonging. The most vigorous social action can be pilloried as partisan self-interest unless it finds foundation in truth that comes from beyond. The exposition of Scripture still has the power to bring down the mighty from their seats and exalt those of low degree.

I make no special claims for the sermons offered here. Indeed, they have been prodded into print by the insistence of friends who should have known better. I have heard enough great preaching in my time to know that these are not.

What I can say on my behalf, however, is that in twenty-five years as a parish and itinerant preacher I have never doubted the efficacy of preaching. I enjoy preaching and I enjoy preparing to preach. The romance of words intrigues me. I find it enormously satisfying to be able to anchor a point with some remembered word or experience that seems to fit with providential precision. The messages that comprise this volume do not illustrate brilliance. They are the result of ordinary gifts and sustained attention. Those with larger endowments of faith, intelligence, and imagination and similar attentiveness would have no trouble doing better.

E. T. C.

CHAPTER 1

The Hardest Blow of All

"I will praise thee for I am fearfully and wonderfully made!"
So exclaimed the writer of the 139th Psalm. Fearfully and
wonderfully made. Just which of man's impressive credentials
prompted this word we do not know. Perhaps it was man's
durability, his capacity for stress, his ability to take it and
keep coming back for more.

Man's body can absorb a lot of punishment: unrelieved
thirst, unwise diet, sleepless nights; the emergency amputation
of a limb without anesthetic, years of backbreaking toil.

Man's mind is no less durable. It can work without letup
for days. It can stretch to receive, store and recall more and
more information. It can adjust to new truth. It can grapple
gamely with paradox and contradiction.

And the heart of man? Here is capacity to absorb shock,
to hover on the brink of despair and recover, to weather loss,
to bear up under the collapse of long-held dreams.

11

Fearfully and wonderfully made. And yet, there is one blow
to which humankind is vulnerable. On the strength of both
personal and pastoral experience one feels justified in calling
this the hardest blow of all. This is the blow that can erase a
man's smile, buckle his knees, stoop his shoulders, snap his
mind and even break his heart. The hardest blow of all is to
be rejected!

Rejection comes in a variety of forms and faces. It can be
real or imagined. One can be rejected by other people. One
can imagine himself rejected by God. One can even reject
his own self.

There is such a thing as vocational rejection. As when a
man is laid off and curtly told that his skill has become an
anachronism in today's world. Kurt Vonnegut, Jr., in his book
God Bless You, Mr. Rosewater, has us focus on a small town
in Ohio, in which a saw-making plant provides the main industry. He writes: "Actually there aren't many sawmakers
left. The saw factory is almost fully automatic now. If you
can work a pinball machine you can run the factory, make
12,000 saws a day." [1]

It is possible for one generation to reject another. As when
a son puts his aging parents on the shelf. As when parents
write off all the teenage culture with a gust of withering scorn.
As when a corporation arbitrarily fires a man at the age of
sixty and replaces him with a man of forty. As when some
bearded know-it-all proclaims his mistrust of everyone over
thirty.

There can be rejection on the grounds of race. Apparently
some people never feel tall enough unless they have other
people under them.

There can be social rejection, a subtle form of caste, where
people are judged and separated according to their parentage,
their ability to amass money and display wealth. Something

like this goes into the feeling that many *New York Times* readers have toward readers of the *Daily News.* "Can any good thing come out of Nazareth?" (John 1:46) they asked in response to the claims of Jesus. And that was that. Social rejection!

And there can be rejection of self, as when a man quits on himself inside, grows to hate his own flesh, and becomes a candidate for suicide.

Just how severe a blow rejection is can be measured in at least two ways. Look first at the lengths to which we go to prevent rejection. Here, I believe, is the root cause of virtually all of our conformity, the fear of being dropped by some group whose esteem and friendship we prize. Rather than risk rejection, we compromise our moral, cultural, or intellectual standards. There are people who drink who do not like to drink, but who are afraid not to drink. There are people who feel obliged to approve of books for which they have no sympathy, because to disapprove would mean rejection by the group. There are people who applaud plays that they have no business applauding, because not to applaud would put them on the outside. There are people who take political positions to which they do not inwardly subscribe only because they are afraid they might be rejected.

The second most stolen book from the New York Public Library system is Emily Post. The most stolen book of all is the *Holy Bible.* It is noteworthy that both books purport to tell us how to stay in relationship—with man and God. The fear of being dropped is a heavy fear indeed.

Even the counterculture is not exempt from the urge to conform. There a smaller public is involved, but it is nonetheless demanding. Somerset Maugham in *The Moon and Sixpence* said, "It is not difficult to be unconventional in the eyes of the world when your unconventionality is but the convention of your set. It affords you then an inordinate amount of self-esteem. You have the self-satisfaction of courage without the inconvenience of danger." [2]

We go to enormous lengths to prevent rejection. Look, moreover, at the strong reactions that rejection touches off. Elston Howard spent most of his active baseball life with the New York Yankees. Astute fans of the sport will remember that towards the end of his career he was traded to Boston. This move jarred the celebrated catcher more than a collision at home plate. A sports writer who is intimate with Elston Howard said, "It was not moving to Boston that upset him. It was just the thought that after so many successful years as a Yankee he was no longer wanted."

Rejection usually touches off a chain reaction that starts with self-pity, moves to sour grapes (who wanted to belong anyway?), goes on to bitterness and finally hardens into thoughts of vengeance. Did you ever try to console a jilted lover?

It is my guess that most of the disturbances we've had in our prisons, and some that have broken out on the boardwalks along the Jersey Shore and in other places in our country recently, are traceable at bottom to the sin of rejection. Always, of course, there are the surface causes, but underneath is the grim fact of rejection.

It is a soul-shattering experience to come upon the words "Keep Out" and know that they are meant for you. Keep out of this school! Keep out of this neighborhood! Keep off this beach! Keep off this job! Some years ago when we were trying to put together a fair housing ordinance in a community in the Midwest, I thought it advisable to meet with realtor members of my church who were opposed to the ordinance. We met, as I remember it, on a quiet Thursday afternoon over coffee. One man led off at a surprisingly naïve level. He said, "You know, Reverend, we discriminate in every aspect of our life. When this church chose you, it failed to choose someone else as minister. When you bought that necktie you chose it out of an assortment and rejected others."

When it came my turn to speak, I had to be firm almost to the point of anger. I pointed out that there is no similarity at all between the rejection of an inanimate necktie and the rejection of people. The essential nature of a necktie is not affected by rejection. A human being has his essence badly altered by rejection. His very manhood is assaulted.

We need each other, and we react strongly, almost demonically, when cut off. No island is a man. We know this. Harry Stack Sullivan said that two great motors of human behavior and thought are the pursuit of satisfactions and the maintenance of security. He went on to say that this security is always threatened when there is a fear of disapproval, a lack of support, or the threat of rejection.

What does the Christian faith have to say about rejection? Well, for one thing, it affirms man's need to live in relationship with others. It is not good that man should be alone. Has it ever struck you as significant that there is no formal, abstract definition of God in the Bible? Rather, God is always presented in Scripture in his various relationships: his relationship to nature, to the nations of the earth, to men and women —"Adam, where art thou?" (Gen. 3:9).

Even more striking is the fact that there is no formal definition of man in the Bible. Man as well as God is disclosed in Scripture, even defined, if you will, in terms of his relationships—hiding, fashioning fig leaves, making idols, worshiping, always in relationship. This is how we know *who* we are and *what* we are. Our estrangement from each other is the clearest indication of our fallenness.

Moreover, the Christian faith proclaims in the face of our

fear of rejection, the steadfast love of God. One of America's favorite cowboys a few years back used to end his performances by saying somewhat breezily, "May the good Lord take a likin' to you"—as though there were some doubt about the constancy of the divine affection. When we turn to the Bible we discover that it is in two parts. These parts are not called section 1 and section 2. They are called the Old Testament (or Covenant) and the New Testament. God's relationship to us is not capricious or whimsical. He has *covenanted* his love toward us. He has pledged to love us with an everlasting love!

The Prodigal Son returns expecting to be rejected. Instead he is accepted by his father, who stands in that story as a paradigm of God. God loves us. We can hear that a thousand times on a quiet Sunday morning to little effect. But when that point comes where we suffer the unspeakable pain of rejection, let the words come back, let the truth come home— God loves us! He accepts us as we are. Our striving is only to accept his acceptance of us.

The most neglected and misunderstood teaching of the Christian faith is the doctrine of justification by faith. The term itself is heavy and the explanations usually given to interpret it heavier still. What justification by faith essentially means is this: that our acceptance with God is not the goal but the starting point of the Christian life. Our acceptance with God is not a thing to be hoped for, or worked for, or striven for. It is what God has already done for us in Christ. Faith is our acceptance, in humility and gratitude, of God's acceptance of us.

What else does the Christian faith have to say about rejection? It presents us with a Savior who himself experienced rejection. "He was despised and rejected of men," said Isaiah (53:3). It is conceivable that that verse initially had reference to a king and perhaps even to the nation itself, but it is inconceivable that that chapter is lacking in all reference to Jesus. "He was despised and rejected of men." He was unwanted by church, by government, by society. He came to his own and his own received him not. He had no place to lay his head. He died on a cross, suspended between heaven and earth, as if wanted by neither. From the cross he cried, "My God, my God, why hast thou forsaken me?" (Matt. 27:46) not so much to bemoan his pain as to express his sense of separation and rejection.

This is more than one of the "inconveniences of greatness," as someone has put it—as though Jesus were rejected only in the sense that he lived ahead of his time. Any Christology that would reduce the feeling of rejection that Jesus knew to a theological fiction is untrue. His rejection was real—every whit as real as ours.

What stands up to arrest our attention is the fact that when he was rejected, Jesus did not react like us. He did not indulge in self-pity. He did not engage in sour grapes. He did not become embittered or stoop to vengeance. The writer of the Epistle to the Hebrews knew the why of it all: "Therefore he had to be made like his brethren in every respect, so that he might become a merciful and faithful high priest in the service of God, to make expiation for the sins of the people. For because he himself has suffered and been tempted, he is able to help those who are tempted" (Heb. 2:17,18, RSV).

Finally, faith has this to say. God in his mercy sets the rejected ones of the earth into a community in which each receives the other as all have been received by God. The climate of any authentic Church is controlled by the love of God. Acceptance is not conditioned upon whether someone qualifies—by the size of his purse, the impressiveness of his achievements, his moral rectitude. The Church that God intended is a community where each receives the other as all have been received by God. He loved us and gave himself for us. As he has loved us, so ought we to love one another.

The invitation is always out to "come as you are." This does not mean that Jesus in receiving us approves of us as we are. Acceptance and approval are not the same. In fact, disapproval can be a form of acceptance.

Frequently, one hears it said that the Church is simply a pragmatic way for people who believe alike to get things done. But Joseph Haroutunian in his book *God With Us* was coming closer to the truth when he said, "They are together (members of a church) not only for accomplishing common purposes but also for being present one to another." [3] That's why we go to church—to be present one to another, to really be there when the other needs us.

A nine-year-old girl said one time in an essay for her teacher, "I don't know exactly what a family is, but I know one thing—your friends can go off and say they don't want to be your friends any more, but people just can't go off and say they don't want to be your family any more." This is what God intends the Church to be: a family in which each receives the other as all have been received by God.

The hardest blow of all is rejection. I talked with the chief engineer on a freighter a while ago who told me that he frequently brings back specimens of God's wild creation for the zoo in his home city in Germany. He spoke about bringing back crocodiles and alligators and poisonous snakes. "How do you do it?" I asked. He replied, "It's very simple. If I have a boa constrictor that I'm bringing home from India, I feed it two or three rabbits. The reptile devours them instantly and then curls up and sleeps until I get it home."

How remarkable! After an animal has had enough to eat, its anxieties cease and it is at peace. But with man, it's different. After we've had enough to eat, and our primary physical satisfactions are attended to, our worries only begin. This is because we are made for each other. One of our cardinal worries has to do with rejection. In fact, the fear of being dropped is so strong with us that we often choose to "stay out," to "wallflower" it, to stay on the edges, because we might get hurt.

It may very well be that some one of you reading this chapter is caught in the depression that rejection always brings. Anger and bitterness may seem the only way.

I have three words for you. God loves you! Jesus understands you! The Church is ready to receive you as you are!

Closing Prayer

Lord, we pray for all who are caught in the
hopeless cycle of rejection, resentment, and
   retaliation.
Let thy saving and delivering word have its
   way among us.
Help us who know thee to be better models of
   thy Love.
Fashion us into a hearing and restoring
fellowship, through the same Jesus Christ
   Our Lord who loved us and gave himself for us.
                      Amen.

CHAPTER 2

Locked in a Room with Open Doors

". . . I have set before you life and death, blessing and curse;
therefore choose life, that you and your descendants may live."
Deuteronomy 30:19, RSV

In renting a modest cottage in the Poconos one summer, we
reaped an unexpected bonus. The previous owner until her
death had been a librarian and there were good books in
tempting profusion in virtually every room in the place. One
that caught my eye was Hans Sachs' volume *Masks Of Love
And Life.* This is a calm and sensible book, but one of its
chapter titles hit me with the force of a jet on takeoff. I can
see it yet: "Locked in a Room with Open Doors."

The story behind that title is told in the chapter's opening
paragraph. Says Sachs, "In a family of my acquaintance were
two brothers, the younger of whom had a dread of open doors.
The older one became impatient, as older brothers will be,
and, wanting to break him of his habit, he threatened: 'One
day I will lock you up in a room with all the doors open.' " [1]

"Locked in a Room with Open Doors." What an image

those words conjure up. If you think about them long enough, they are likely to make your palms moist and create strange feelings of uneasiness within. They suggest that a man can be immobilized by inner weaknesses as well as outer obstacles. To be sure, there are people in our society who are locked in a room with *shut* doors. That's what most of the noise is about these days—people trying to open doors: doors to more adequate education, doors to decent jobs, to good health, to better housing, to a fairer share of political and economic power. I, for one, am glad that the Christian church in this country has found its muscle and is helping to propel the battering ram forward. In a democracy closed doors are indefensible. Under our Constitution, life, liberty, and the pursuit of happiness are guaranteed to all.

But it is precisely when broad-gauged social action programs are in full swing that we are most likely to overlook—even resent—the fact that man can still be a prisoner when all the doors are open. The enemies are not all out there. Some are on the inside. It is so easy to fall into the habit of blaming our unrealized selves on outside forces. The mood of the day might well be caught up in a paraphrase of one of Shakespeare's better known lines, "The fault, dear Brutus, is not in ourselves, but in our systems that we are miserable." Systems indeed can be oppressive. None is perfect. None is likely to be perfect. Yet, under God, we have a mandate to improve the systems and remove as many of the impediments to freedom as we can. No reduction of obstacles on the outside, however, can guarantee freedom within.

R. E. C. Brown suggests that there are two ways of viewing sin: "The refusal to control what can be controlled, and the attempt to control what cannot be controlled." [2] When we assume an essentially passive stance to life we are guilty of refusing to control what can be controlled. It is not a kindness to suggest to any individual or people that they may absolve themselves of all initiative and responsibility.

Back in the summer of 1962, the Police Athletic League sought to raise money in New York City by circulating a poster depicting a destitute youngster who was obviously in for a long hot summer. The tag line underneath said: "If You Don't Care, Why Should He?" I suggest that this is a dangerous kind of appeal. There are reasons why the lad should care whether I care or not: because he has the irrepressible gift of life, because he has the power of choice, and because he has the will to fashion at least part of what he feels.

Samuel Johnson was right when he said,

> How small, of all that human hearts endure,
> That part which laws or kings can cause or cure!
> Still to ourselves in every place consign'd
> Our own felicity we make or find.[3]

"Locked in a Room with Open Doors." Some are locked in from life by hatred. They are prisoners of the spirit of vengeance, unable to shake the urge to get even. Hate is a cruel master. It hurts the hater as much as the "hatee." Nothing durable has ever been built in our society on hate.

The current racial unrest in this country poses some very serious problems here. There can be no social progress without indignation. Moreover, unless this indignation is organized and directed, it will not prevail. When righteous indignation is thus organized, polarization is inevitable—in the church, in the home, in society. We should not shy away so long as we see polarization as a middle step. A line must be drawn and opposing sides identified before meaningful debate can take place. The trick is to be able to become sufficiently aroused and indignant without allowing deep feelings of per-

sonal hatred to set in. By hating we become like that which
we are seeking to exorcise.

Hate feeds on stereotypes. It has to continually shut out
certain truths and experiences in order to maintain its fire. A
critic who shall remain nameless was honest enough to say
one time in commenting on a performing artist: "Something
I wrote about him once so prejudiced me against him that I
can't enjoy anything he does."

Jesus said plainly that we are to love our enemies and pray
for those who "despitefully use" us (Matt. 5:44). We are
forever coming up against those words and telling ourselves
that he really didn't mean *our* enemies. Ours are always different, special, particularly diabolical. But, of course, he did
mean our enemies. As Christians we are to deal with others
as God has dealt with us.

"Locked in a Room with Open Doors." Some of us are
locked in by worry. What James Thurber said of Harold Ross
may be said of many of us: "He lived at the corner of work
and worry." [4] There is such a thing as secure poverty. This
is the poverty of little children in deprived homes who, even
though they feel the pinch of want, have security in believing
that somehow, some way, their parents will provide. But there
is also in our country and surely in the world at large what
might be called insecure poverty. Such poverty exists among
the fathers and mothers who must do the providing for their
families and are driven frantic by the fact that they cannot.
It would be fatuous of us to suggest that all worry about
money and income is unworthy of faith. A certain minimal
level of income is required if one is to be lifted above the
grubbing and drudging stage of life. But I'm thinking of those
of us who have passed that level, myself included, and seem
not to know when to stop—those who are always salivating
for more, always anxious, always perturbed, forever feeling

that they don't have enough. To turn life into one unrelenting hustle is to remain locked in a room even though all the doors are open. Up to a point our acquisitions and possessions can liberate. After that, they tend to clog and jam our lives. This is why a sage prophet once suggested that each of us needs at least one good fire in his lifetime.

A mystic from India was being introduced to New York City. His guide, with more nerve than wisdom, took him down to the Times Square subway station at the peak of a morning rush hour. The visitor was appalled at what he saw—people with attaché cases pushing hard and driving madly. He could only think to ask, "Is there a wolf behind them?" "No," said his friend, "there's a dollar in front of them!"

Will Durant was right. "A life devoted to the acquisition of wealth is useless unless we know how to turn it into joy; and this is an art that requires culture and wisdom. A succession of sensual pursuits never satisfies for long; one must understand the ends of life as well as the art of acquiring means. Men are a thousand times more intent on becoming rich than on acquiring culture, though it is quite certain that what a man *is* contributes more to his happiness than what he *has*." [5]

Jesus commended us to the faithfulness of God. Is that really too simple for us to come down to? "Take no thought for your life, what ye shall eat, or what ye shall drink" (Matt. 6:25a). Is it not possible that we have acquired too many necessities that aren't really necessary? Maltbie D. Babcock said of Jesus: "Anxiety has no place in the life of one of God's children. Christ's serenity was one of the most unmistakable signs of his filial trust. He was tired and hungry and thirsty and in pain; but we cannot imagine him anxious or fretful. His mind was kept in perfect peace because it was stayed on God." [6]

Some of us stay locked in a room with open doors because we are afraid of the new. Every so often one sees in the paper where a man who has served his term in prison goes out and violates some minor law so that he might return to jail where the perimeters are fixed and the routine is familiar. I am told that when you take goldfish out of the bowls in which we usually keep them and turn them loose in a pond, they will continue to swim in small circles for quite a while. They are afraid of the new.

We are afraid of new experiences. Sachs, in the chapter we started off with, says, "The world is open for travel in all directions, but the well-trodden thoroughfares are generally preferred to fascinating nooks and by-ways." [7] A friend of mine who teaches theology got caught up in a tourist group going across Europe. He was struck by the fact that one couple in particular could think of nothing more to say when confronted with the new than "That's just like ours," or, "That's not like ours"—as though the little experiences that they had tracked were the norm by which to judge everything else in the world. This is to live deductively when we might live inductively, taking on each new experience as it comes without fear.

We are afraid of new people. We see in new people a threat to the equilibrium we have managed to establish in our management of life. At a delegated convention, following the meal, the master of ceremonies twiddled the crowd. He said, "I know you are enjoying yourselves. You made a point of sitting with your own group to be sure that you would have a good time." They had come to the convention in groups. They were rooming on the same floor of the hotel as groups. And they were taking their meals at the convention as groups. This is to fear new people.

Instinctively we gravitate to those we know. But there is

growth and expansion and education awaiting us in those
whom we do not know. Good things might happen if we
could discipline ourselves, for instance, Sunday after Sunday to speak to two people at church that we do not know
before we speak to someone that we do.

But the most oppressive lock-in of all centers in *our fear
of new ideas*. After all, we have worked out our faith and,
such as it is, we do not wish to have it disturbed. It's something like the mother with ten children who sighs at nine in
the evening when they are all tucked quietly in bed. She
doesn't want any of them kicking off the covers and spoiling
the calm. We fear exposure to the new. I am not suggesting
that we ought to question the fundamental conviction that we
have met God in Jesus Christ. I'm thinking rather of what we
make of that experience—how we interpret it, how we say
it, how we live it, how we apply it.

We are guilty of striving to be justified by consistency
rather than by faith. In a pluralistic, technological, revolutionary age no man can expect to get it right the first time every
time.

Years ago when Mike Wallace began to make a name ior
himself he built a reputation as a hard interrogator. I can
still see him as he sat there with sheets of notes and confronted the "lamb" in the other chair whose articles and
utterances he had scrupulously studied. Wallace would lean
over and say, "Sir, you once said—" The guest would begin
to climb about in his mind to see if he could recall what he
had said years and years ago. There was even a story going
around that Mike Wallace in the life to come would sit down
in the presence of the Almighty and say, "Sir, you once said
in Genesis—" The implication behind this line of questioning
is that anyone who is worth his salt intellectually ought to be
consistent. In my opinion there is more honesty in the kind

of intellectual leadership that has the courage to revise itself as life moves on.

Some of us have remained uncommitted on large questions out of a fear of taking a position that we will not be able to maintain. We sit back waiting and waiting. What draws us to men like Karl Barth, Malcolm X, Harvey Cox, and James Pike is the courage they mustered to revise themselves. "Sir, you once said—" "Yes, I did, but I have since received more light." Begin to think about sex education in the public schools now. If you arrive at conclusions that will have to be changed five or six years from now, in the name of God, change them. Let's be done with the imagined need for consistency that keeps us locked up in a cell when all the doors are open.

Some of us are so rigid that we look like a doll without joints. Rabbi Mark Goldman of Temple Emmanuel (New York City) announced an intriguing sermon title not long ago: "U-Turns Permitted." Wherever did we get the idea that once we conceived a point of view we had to defend it to the death? U-turns are not only permitted, my friends, they are encouraged; yea, they are demanded of us. One of the key terms of the Old Testament is the term *shubh* which means turn. Turn to me. Turn away from the false to the true. Moses said to the people as he neared his death and they neared their Promised Land, "And when all these things come upon you, the blessing and the curse, which I have set before you, and you call them to mind among all the nations where the Lord your God has driven you, and *return* to the Lord your God, then God . . . will have compassion . . . and . . . bring you into the land" (Deut. 30:1–5, RSV).

There are doors on the outside that need to be opened. But this is only one front. The other front centers in the doors within our own selves that keep us stopped and stymied. Nathaniel Hawthorne understood this uneasiness: "What other

dungeon is so dark as one's own heart! What jailer so in-
exorable as one's self!" [8]

But there is good news for us. If we are locked in, we need
not stay there. Besides the inner misery that makes us want to
get out, there is the call of God that summons us out. "I have
set before you," he said to the Israelites and he says to us,
"life and death, blessing and curse, therefore choose life,
that you and your descendants may live." Jesus came to preach
release to the captives and since it is not recorded that he very
frequently went to jail to physically liberate people we are
permitted to conclude that he was intent on liberating men
from the fears and hang-ups of their own hearts.

I have read most everything William Temple wrote, but
nothing this towering churchman ever penned means more
to me than his devotional comment on Jesus' statement, "I am
the way." Says Temple, speaking of the way, "It starts where
each one stands. We do not have to find its starting place. It
starts here where we are." [9] Christ is the way. *As* you are,
what you are, and *where* you are, he will meet you and lead
you out.

Closing Prayer

O Thou who art the author of liberty,
Forgive us the constricted and
    fear-filled existence that we settle
    for when we might have life.

By a knowledge of our misery and
    the awareness of thy beckoning grace
Lead us out, that we may serve thee
    in the freedom of love.
Through Jesus Christ Our Lord.
                                    Amen.

CHAPTER 3

Follow Me

*When a minister has a keynote message in his bones, Home-*coming Sunday is surely the time to turn it loose. The summer is past. A new season beckons. Anticipation runs high.

But what can a man say to a troubled church, in a troubled city, in a troubled world. Pep rally rhetoric is for university campuses. Crash programs and the promise of instant cures belong to Batten, Barton, Durstin, and Osborne—not to Matthew, Mark, Luke, and John.

Thick volumes of social analysis are the province of research fellows who have lucked into a foundation grant. Throwing in the towel is no possibility for those who have been given a towel and commissioned to serve.

What can a man say? He can lift up and commend two words of Jesus that resonate with relevance for men today: "Follow me."

Jesus uttered these words not once but many times: to Peter and Andrew by the Sea of Galilee; to Levi, the son of Alphaeus at the seat of customs. To a balking inquirer Jesus' words were, "Let the dead bury their dead and come, follow me"; to the rich young ruler, "Sell what you have, give to the poor and come, follow me." And to all in his time and in succeeding times, "If any man would come after me, let him deny himself and take up his cross and follow me."

These words of entreaty and command are plain and disconcertingly personal. They cut through a maze of theology. They are no respecter of denominational ties or ecclesiastical lines. They do not bow to rank or privilege. They are tall enough and deep enough to guide a church in the most ambiguous of times.

There are several considerations that have moved me in recent months to a new appreciation of these words. First, anyone who says, "Follow me," is going someplace—and we need direction. These words strike us initially as unwelcome and intrusive. They threaten to dislocate us. But ponder them longer and find that part of their appeal lies in the fact that *they promise to connect us with one who is going someplace.*

The therapy of hibernation, so widely practiced by so many in our time, cannot really heal what hurts us deep inside. Yet, leadership that knows where it is going is hard to come by in our society; and so, we hibernate. There was more truth than humor to the legend I spotted on a T-shirt in New Hampshire a few summers back: "Don't follow me, I'm lost!" One of our more vocal public leaders was criticized the other day by a veteran politician who spoke his mind frankly: "I don't take him seriously because I don't think he is going anyplace."

Jesus has a plan, a work to do, a purpose to achieve in history and beyond. And he deigns to cut us in. The word that is translated *follow* in most instances in the gospel is rooted in the Greek word for road. To follow is to share the same road. The Christian's prayer is not for a longer stay with God but for a closer walk with God.

Moreover, anyone who says, "Follow me," is obviously more interested in the future than the past—and we need a loyalty to the future. With Jesus it's not where you've been that matters, but where you're going; not whether you have fallen, but whether you will get up; not whom you've hurt in the past, but whom you will help in the future.

A relatively new approach to psychiatry has been abroad for a few years now under the name Reality Therapy. Its founding mentor was William Glasser. The approach makes sense to me. Reality therapists insist that it is futile to keep on rummaging around in a man's past, getting people to articulate and amplify yesterday's failures and to recall how the world has mistreated them. The important thing is to get them to face their needs and prepare for a future worth living.

This approach may err a bit on the side of oversimplification, but I find myself saying "Amen" when Glasser writes: "Without denying that the patient had an unsatisfactory past, we find that to look for what went wrong does not help him. What good comes from discovering that you are afraid to assert yourself because you had a domineering father? Both patient and therapist can be aware of this historical occurrence; they can discuss it in all of its ramifications for years, but the knowledge will not help the patient assert himself now." [1]

Fan through the pages of the gospel record and you will be startled to discover how little time Jesus spent allowing people to expand on a burdened past. When the woman taken in adultery was thrust into his presence he did not try to explore the circumstances that had pushed her to her fall. He simply took her by the hand and said, "Go thy way and sin no more" (John 8:11). When Nicodemus came to him under the cover of night, shackled by an impossible legalism, Jesus didn't ask him how he got that way but said simply, "You must be born again" (John 3:3).

The story of the Prodigal Son may indeed be the paradigm that indicates how God deals with men and women who have failed. The younger brother in the far country never got to recite before his father the speech that he had so carefully learned and memorized. Instead, his words were smothered in his father's love. He was given a ring for his finger, a robe for his back, and shoes for his feet, and restored to full status as a son. For to be penitent is to be forgiven, and to be forgiven is to rise up and follow.

Yes, we might fall again. We do not move on brashly for our failures are still very much in our minds. But we know that we are being led by light and love. This is what the eminent New Testament scholar T. W. Manson was testifying to when he said: "The living Christ still has two hands, one to point the way, and the other held out to help us along. So the Christian ideal lies before us, not as a remote and austere mountain peak, an ethical Everest which we must scale by our own skill and endurance; but as a road on which we may walk with Christ as guide and friend. And we are assured, as we set out on the journey, that he is with us always, 'even unto the end of the world' " (Matt. 28:20).[2]

Finally, consider the fact that whoever commands us to follow and wins our allegiance has given us a norm by which to test our living. Christ does not absorb us or intend to absorb us. There is a distance between the Lord and the servant, so that our selfhood, integrity, and individuality might be preserved. Moreover, he calls us not to slavish imitation but to follow—each of us in the context of his time and place. There is no time or place or circumstance where one cannot follow.

What Christian living is all about, singly or corporately, is following Christ—an important thing for us to see at this particular time in the life of our nation and church when we are being prodded by the living Lord to move with history. "Follow me"—this is the word that ought to monitor what we do and say and think as trustees, deacons, committee members, council members, ministers, and members of the congregation. Is this action, this decision, this policy, this attitude of such a quality that it is moving our church in the direction Jesus is going? We may not always agree on what it means to follow Jesus, but we cannot question the fundamental presumption that we are here to follow Jesus. This is the acid test stripped of its theological decor.

It's safe to tell it now. A few days after John F. Kennedy was assassinated a member of the church I was serving in Ann Arbor called and suggested that the one thing we might do to partially redeem the tragedy would be to provide Marina Oswald with an opportunity to improve her English. Mrs. Oswald had expressed a desire to stay in the United States and learn its language better. Because it would have been unwise to bring this before the entire congregation, a few of us who represented the executive committee of that church got in touch with Marina Oswald.

To make a long story short, in due time and in cooperation with the FBI and others, Marina Oswald came to Ann Arbor. She slipped into our community at night by train while a battery of reporters were waiting hawkishly at the airport. She lived with a modest family that takes seriously its devotion to God and its love for people. When we were finally pressed to do so, we joined the University of Michigan in issuing a modest press release. The mail began to come in. There were some who were quick and hot to say that what we did was unpatriotic. Others told us that our action was unwise, still others that it was unfair. (One woman said that she had belonged to a church for forty years and what it had done for her in all that time she could write on the back of a postage stamp.) Others were prompted to say that what we did was grossly un-American. I answered every letter, rightly or wrongly feeling it the obligation of my ministry to do so. I said in effect to each person who criticized, "The one thing you haven't shown us is that what we have done is unlike Christ."

It doesn't really matter whether an action is profitable or popular, whether it is practical or realistic, whether it wins a salute from a city or nation. What matters only and always is whether it can be understood as following Jesus Christ.

As a Presbyterian, I stood a few inches taller in the fall of 1970 when I read what the General Assembly of the Presbyterian Church of South Africa said to the prime minister of that country. The World Council of Churches had decided to give financial aid to several black African liberation movements, including some listed in South Africa as terrorist organizations. Because of this stand, the government asked the churches of South Africa to pull out of the World Council of Churches. The answer of the General Assembly was: "The Assembly reminds the prime minister that its only Lord and master is Jesus Christ and it may not serve other masters and that its task is not necessarily to support the government in power but to be faithful to the gospel." [3]

"Follow me." To follow Jesus is to have a plan. To follow Jesus is to face and embrace the future. To follow Jesus is to have a star by which to steer. Every time he comes across our way and bids us follow, he creates a crisis. And we can never be the same again. For when that command registers on our souls, we can choose to die to God and live to self, or to die to self and live to God.

The kind of loyalty I should like to command of myself and see congregations offer up to God can be summed up in the words of an obscure figure in the Old Testament by the name of Ittai who belonged to a foreign country. On a dark day when many of David's troops were choosing to desert their chief, David turned to Ittai and said, in effect: "You've got it made at home. Why don't you go back? You've served us well." But Ittai answered: "As the Lord liveth, and as my lord the king liveth, surely in what place my lord the king shall be, whether in death or life, even there also will thy servant be" (2 Sam. 15:21).

Closing Prayer

O God, if we follow at a distance or not at all;
If we follow from a sense of duty void of passion;
If we follow only when it is convenient;
Speak to us in commanding love,
And help us to become what we were meant to be.
Through Jesus Christ Our Lord.

Amen.

CHAPTER 4

From the Many to the One

". . . but this one thing I do . . ."

Philippians 3:13

In April 1970 the Methodist magazine Response *was kind* enough to carry an article of mine which suggested that the decade ahead would be a time for traveling light. Soon after the piece appeared I received a letter from a woman in a Midwestern state. I should like to share it with you now, first, to show that people will occasionally find in a message directives that were not intended; and, second, because the sentiment expressed in the letter conveys a mood that most of us have flirted with at one time or another:

> Dear Sir:
> We are taking your advice—"Choose Life and Travel Light"—as it appeared in the April issue of *Response.*
> We are selling our house and furniture and moving into a camper, so all our possessions will be contained in that. And we're moving—we intend to see the country. Our mail will

be sent to General Delivery in the next small town. We'll be members of no particular church, club, or organization. No more meetings, no more committees—we've had it up to here.

We've both been active in the local church and conference, but we've found that they can get along very well without us. You're only needed when you produce the way the man in charge wants you to. Any ideas of yours are nil.

Your advice came as a fresh drink of water. Run away, who doesn't? Everyone runs from something. The young people hate possessions, but they have their hot little hands out for our money and help.

So if you see one more trailer on the road—it's us.

Which of us has not longed to pull up stakes and take to the open road? Which of us has not chafed under the demands of whatever system it is that puts clothing on our back and bread on our table? Which of us has not yearned to shuck those close-fitting responsibilities and be free? Come now, haven't you at least *priced* a camper?

What touches me most about that letter is its sincerity. One senses regret between the lines, a wish that things hadn't gone that way. The writer had given it a good try. Perhaps she was tired. Nothing looks good to us, even the work of God, when we are exhausted. It has been rather well established that 25 percent of the people in a congregation give 75 percent of the money. My judgment would be that it's equally true that 25 percent of the people in a congregation do 75 percent of the work.

Let those of us who lead causes, whether within or without the church, take warning from this incident not to exploit the willing. It is possible to burn good people out before their time. The violin bow always taut will soon lose its resiliency.

At any rate, the woman decided that she would now go in for generalized living as opposed to particularized living:

nature over people, travel over roots, campfires over committees. Right at our elbow all the time is the temptation to live
extensively instead of intensively. We would like to climb
every mountain and sail every sea, drive every road, fly every
plane, sip every wine, taste every delicacy, visit every country,
see every play, watch every athlete, read every book, leaf
through every magazine, hear every joke, and catch every
movie.

Edmond Cahn speaks to this hankering at a deeper level
with some psychiatric insight: "None of us is wholly content
with the casual confinements of a single career, a single sex,
a single lifetime and concatenation of scenery. Each desires
to live out all kinds of lives, to exert all powers and receive
all adulations, to suffer and enjoy every sort of passion, to
possess all the women that ever yielded or refused to yield—
in short, to play the Faust in an endless metempsychosis of
exploits and triumphs. The compulsive lusts drive the self out
beyond the boundaries of its own body and send it to enact
comedies, tragedies, tableaux, and epics elsewhere." [1]

At times we all want to move away from our problems and
set up shop somewhere else. Nothing humbles me more than
my attempts at the crossword puzzle in the *Sunday Times*
each week. My strategy is to begin in the upper lefthand
section until I mess it up. Then I move to the upper right and
drop down the right side to the lower right corner. Then to
the lower left and up. I live with the illusion that when I get
stuck somewhere I can move on and start over indefinitely.
Always, however, I am eventually forced to face the fact that
the puzzle is one piece. To keep moving away from life's
difficult situations only postpones payday, it does not cancel it.

We need association in depth with other people over and
beyond the kinship of immediate family. Cicero knew this
years ago: "If a wise man were granted a life of abundance

of everything material, so that he had leisure to contemplate everything worth knowing, still could he not communicate with another human being he would abandon life." Certainly Jesus in a hundred different ways stressed the importance of relationships over going places and collecting things.

But people who sour on living responsible lives usually suffer from more than fatigue. Chances are they expected too much and thus became disappointed. General aspirations are seldom fully realized in particular situations. We mistakenly expect our concrete relationships to embody the best features of a dozen similar relationships that we have known or heard about. That is, we pursue a composite image that is out of touch with reality. We fantasize impossible combinations out of the best that we have known and then expect one particular home or church or job to produce it all.

The rule suggests itself that when we pass from the many to the one, that is, when we move from broad generalizations to specific life situations—when we pass from the many to the one—we cannot expect that *one* to possess all the best features of the *many*.

Think of marriage and the home. As a man matures he comes to know a variety of women—his mother, his nurse, his sisters, cousins, teachers, neighbors, and so on. And if he is a fairly normal young man he will probably "play the field" in his dating. But it is altogether critical when he passes from the many to the one that he not expect his bride to combine the finest qualities of all the other women he has known.

He can't have Mary's looks and Helen's personality; Martha's tenderness and Laura's figure; Betty's money and Carol's brains; and Virginia's parents. And, of course, it works the other way around for the expectations of the bride for her husband. In the Methodist service of marriage the question is put to the man: "Wilt thou have this woman to be thy wedded wife and forsaking all others (singly or in combination) keep thee only unto her?"

This is the crisis moment, when the man passes from the many to the one. His concern is no longer with femininity, or womanhood at large, but with this one woman, this person. Some men remain bachelors all their days rather than face the trauma of moving from the many to the one. The late Theodore Reik said, only half in jest: "Beware of bachelors who have an idealistic view of noble chaste womanhood. Young women should prefer the company of declared woman-haters. They always marry." [2]

We must pass from the many to the one because this is how we grow. Our best efforts are not to be directed toward children in general but these children, ours; not toward the management of homes in general, but this home; love beamed not toward women in general but toward this woman (this man) in this place.

George Santayana tells in his book *Persons and Places* of his father's fondness for a line from Quintilian: "For exploring human nature one household is large enough." [3] Surely our Lord would have us respect the individuality of the partner we choose. To bring impossible expectations into a marriage is to saddle the home with what psychiatrists call an "infantile inclusion."

Or think of the point as it relates to work. There is an enormous amount of vocational unrest in our society. So many people want out of where they are. So many ministers want out of the churches that they serve. So many bureaucrats want out. Some jobs are admittedly drudgery day by day, but let us not forget that there is drudgery in every man's job.

The young have a way of generalizing about vocations. It was no trick at all for me at age fourteen to hold in one small mind the possibilities of being a cowboy, a baseball player, and a news reporter. Youth is the time to generalize, to fantasize about one, two, three or more possible careers. Eventually, as life moves on, we *must* pass from the many to the one—unless we are afflicted with the "perpetual student" syndrome which keeps us uncommitted far too long.

When we finally get down to one vocation, expressed in one particular place, we tend then to invoke the myth of the composite and thus become unduly restless with what we have. We would like to have the expense account of a salesman, the vacation of a teacher, the glamor of an actress, the prestige of a president, the income of a doctor, the hours of a plumber, and the independence of a judge.

What we don't think about is how long the doctor studied to get where he is. What we don't think about is how the plumber longs for higher social status. What we don't think about is the briefcase the judge totes home on the Long Island Rail Road every night. What we don't think about are the hours of rehearsal that the actress grinds out day by day.

There is more vocational mobility in our society now. Men and women in the Armed Forces can get out at the age of forty-three or forty-five and start new careers, but there is still a limit to this kind of movement. We cannot continue to make unlimited moves from one job to another, always imagining that somewhere else we could be more happily employed.

When we stop thinking mythologically and extensively and instead think more realistically and intensively, we can ask God to put a spire on our work. If only we could see what we do where we are as a crucial ministry for him!

> Forenoon, and afternoon, and night!
> The empty song repeats itself. No more!

> Yea, that is Life: make this forenoon sublime,
> This afternoon a psalm, this night a prayer,
> And Time is conquered, and thy crown is won.[4]

Think of the point as it relates to faith. A man can appear awfully devout as a religious generalist. I suppose when we are young we should be to some extent religious generalists. We should be devouring books on comparative religion, visiting other churches, listening to other traditions, comparing, weighing, thinking to decide. But all of this will add up to relatively insignificant prologue unless we pass from the many to the one.

A. E. Taylor has reminded us that "there is nothing heroic about keeping the mind open on all questions simply because we are too indolent to give ourselves the trouble of shutting a door. Nor is it well to leave all doors indiscriminately open, for, though the door often provides an avenue for the entrance of much that is welcome, it also, as we too often forget, affords an exit through which what we can least afford to lose may disappear. The important thing is to judge which doors should be left open and which should be shut." [5]

It is possible to offer God the incense of our admiration while withholding the obedience of our hearts. This is what Masefield was getting at in *The Everlasting Mercy* when he said:

> But trained men's minds are spread so thin
> They let all sorts of darkness in;
> Whatever light man finds they doubt it,
> They love, not light, but talk about it.[6]

Perhaps this helps to explain the phenomenal growth in the belief in astrology in our time. Why not? The stars offer us purported guidance without demanding obedience. What's more, we can study a horoscope without having to be thrown into association or communion with other people.

What made St. Paul the stellar Christian that he was, was the fact that after having been a religiously active man in many ways for many years he submitted to the singular claims of the living Christ: "This one thing I do." He is no longer a generalist, a mere inquirer. Once self-directed, he is now God-directed: "Forgetting what lies behind and straining forward to what lies ahead, I press on toward the goal for the prize of the upward call of God in Christ Jesus" (Phil. 3:13–14, RSV).

How sad, we are inclined to say, that a man who might have been more extensive in his knowledge had he given his ripened years to continuing investigation should suddenly stop with Jesus. But shed no tears for him. Mastery is always achieved through resolved limitation. The man to be pitied is the man who believes in everything just a little bit, the miscellaneous man who has never brought the tattered fragments of his life under the command of a single voice, or gathered his abilities around a single passion.

What is even more interesting about St. Paul, though, is that his magnificent obsession with Christ threw him into a new succession that involved him with particular people in particular places. Had campers been available in St. Paul's time he would at least have looked over the ads in the paper, for he had his troubles with people. It would have been much easier to leave Corinth, for example, than to try to communicate with those ingrates in the church there.

John Calvin, who has a way of steeling our nerve, comments on another portion of Paul's letter to the Philippians. Speaking about men in the ministry who think they could do wonders somewhere else he notes:

It might be in your power to live elsewhere in greater opulence, but God has bound you to the Church, which affords you but a very moderate sustenance: you might elsewhere have more honour, but God has assigned you a situation, in which you live in humble style: you might have elsewhere a more salubrious sky, or a more delightful region, but it is here that your station is appointed. You might wish to have to do with a more humane people: you feel offended with their ingratitude, or barbarity, or pride; in short, you have no sympathy with the disposition or the manners of the nation in which you are but you must struggle with yourself, and do violence in a manner to opposing inclinations, that you may keep by the trade you have got; for you are not free, or at your own disposal. In fine, forget yourself, if you would serve God.[7]

We ministers are guilty of playing with the myth of the composite. Many discouraged ministers whom I know have a picture in their minds of the best of all the churches they have ever visited or served. They like the air-conditioning of one church, the choir of another, the folksiness of a third, the salary of another, the study leave of still another. How long will we torment ourselves with such appeals to fiction!

On the members' side there are people in every congregation who finger this myth of the composite. New York's Riverside Church can't have the rural intimacies of a little church somewhere in a hamlet in Ohio. There are things that one church can do that other churches can't. Instead of trying to realize what is impossible, is it not the better part of wisdom to move from the many to the one wherever we might happen to be, accepting the mix of assets and liabilities, the pluses and minuses, there to serve God with as much vitality as we can command?

When we pass from the many to the one, we can't expect that one to possess all the best features of the many. It belongs to our maturity as human beings—not to mention our maturity as Christians—to move from the many to the one. Unless the good lady who wrote that letter is of retirement age, she is regressing, moving back from the one to the many.

What is love if not locally expressed? What is vocation if not something done in a specific place? What is faith if its object is not singular, if it does not tie us to a given fellowship?

God's love is the model—a love that came down to earth, that got all tangled up in the particularities of our history. For God did not choose to save us by writing in the sky, but by the gift of a child, a man, a cross, and an empty tomb. Let us trust our sample of life. We haven't got it all, but no one has. Let us run not some imagined, ideal race, but as the writer of Hebrews put it, "the race that is set before us"—helps, hindrances and all (Heb. 12:1b).

Closing Prayer

O Thou who didst not disdain to set
    Thy love and do Thy work in the
    midst of men,
keep us faithful to the gospel where
    we are;
lest in dreaming of times and places
    more ideal
    we should fail Thee here and now.
As thou hast loved,
so may we love.
    Through Jesus Christ Our Lord.
                Amen.

CHAPTER 5

The Craving for Clarity

"If you are the Christ, tell us plainly."

John 10:24b, RSV

Some wag in a moment of pique declared that every profession was a conspiracy against the layman. He went on to elaborate by suggesting that lawyers keep us dependent on their services by embalming the law in "legalese," a mix of ancient English and encrusted Latin; that doctors keep us in our place by using long and technical words to describe our ailments; that scientists keep the little man at bay by resorting to symbols and language that only the initiate can understand. And, what is important for our purposes, that theologians and ministers in particular, and the church in general, keep themselves in business by deliberately confounding the simple verities of religion: faith, hope, and love.

This last charge is not unlike the charge that was leveled at Jesus that day in the temple. It was winter and he and his followers sought the shelter of Solomon's porch. The Feast of Dedication was being celebrated. Suddenly Jesus found himself hemmed in by angry Jews who turned upon him and said, "How long will you keep us in suspense? If you are the Christ, tell us plainly." This word "plainly" is one of John's favorite words; he uses it nine times in his gospel. It means "without the obscurity of a parable," "openly and publicly." "If you are the Christ, tell us plainly."

This question might have been raised to bait Jesus, to have him declare himself categorically so that an arrest could be made. On the other hand, the request might have been born out of a deep desire to understand who he was. Let us be generous and concede the second motive.

But Jesus would not oblige! The lack of communication implied in their question did not lie in his inability to tell but in their inability to hear. It is true that nowhere in his earthly ministry did he say to these people flatly, "I am the Christ." He didn't wish to do this, in part because it might have led to crucifixion prematurely; and in part because the term Christ or Messiah had been given so many different meanings that he might have been misunderstood. We cannot really answer another man's *question* until we understand the other man's *meaning* of that question.

On the other hand, Jesus had referred to himself as the bread of life, the water of life, the son of man, the good shepherd, the light of the world. He had done many mighty works. He had forgiven sin. "If Thou art the Christ, tell us plainly." Apparently he had been plain enough for James and John and Peter and Andrew, plain enough for Mary of Magdala, the demoniac of Gadara, Zacchaeus, for Mary and Martha of Bethany and a host of others.

Communication is not achieved by clarity alone. The question of one's affinity for truth is also in the picture. We come at truth with a mind set either to receive or to reject. Jesus

spoke in parables so that those who wished to hear might
hear, and those who had no disposition to hear could not.
Notice these words from the eighth chapter of St. Luke, "To
you it has been given," said Jesus to the disciples, "to know
the secrets of the kingdom of God; but for others they are in
parables, so that seeing they may not see, and hearing they
may not understand" (Luke 8:10, RSV).

We must meet truth part way. We must come to it with
readiness, expectation, and imagination, and the willingness to
participate in it. We suffer in our society from a lack of
imagination. The poet W. H. Auden has traced the blame for
this to the advent of television. In the old days of radio one
had to meet the program part way. I had my mental image
of what Amos and Andy looked like and you had yours. I
had my picture of the Lone Ranger and you had yours. We
met the program part way. But with television, it is all there
before us, and the imagination goes to sleep. We are not
induced, except on rare occasions, to participate. Jesus in
effect is saying, "The truth about who I am has been sounded
but you have not heard." One thinks of a tourist in the Metropolitan Museum standing before a masterpiece and saying, "I
don't see anything in that." Another tourist whispers in reply,
"Don't you wish you could?" "If you are the Christ, tell us
plainly." The answer is clear: "When you are ready to hear,
you will."

This same demand for clarity is made on the church, and
not without justification. "If he is the Christ, tell us plainly.
Our times are out of joint. We are hungry for a word. If he is
the Christ, tell us plainly." It is in order that the church
repent for having failed to declare the message of Jesus Christ
with greater clarity. We have developed a jargon that speaks
to those on the inside but says little to the man outside.

Did you ever sit down in the wee hours of Christmas Eve to assemble a toy that you had purchased for one of the children? A note on the carton declares that a child could put it together in five minutes. You come upon a sleazy diagram that looks as though it were the last copy coughed up by a tired A. B. Dick machine at the end of a long run. "Tell us plainly," you whisper hopefully. And the instructions come: "Take crossbar A and fasten to upright C, keeping the flanged edge to the lower center. Tighten Ferguson bolt making sure lock washer is facing bar B. Insert bracing rod into opening C making sure corner braces are at 90° angles to tube D. Snap end rods in place by pressing with thumb at point A-2. Attach wheels as marked."

The world turns to the church and says, "If he is the Christ, tell us plainly." Karl Barth answers with eleven thick volumes of *Church Dogmatics*. Tillich answers with three closely reasoned volumes of theology. Bultmann answers with two volumes of *New Testament Theology* and a complicated work on demythologizing. "Tell us plainly." They ask for bread and we give them a stone, they ask for fish and we give them a scorpion.

Perhaps most of the blame lies with those of us who are ministers at the local level, for it is part of our job to understand what the theologians are saying, to break their language down, and to share it with our people. Unfortunately, we pastors are frequently as obtuse as the theologians. I remember the feeling of letdown that overtook me when the father of the bride slipped me a book following his daughter's wedding. It was entitled *Write Clearly, Speak Effectively*. How did he know, he had never heard me preach!

T. S. Eliot comments on this precarious business of word selection when he writes in "Burnt Norton":

. . . . Words strain,
Crack and sometimes break, under the burden,
Under the tension, slip, slide, perish,
Decay with imprecision, will not stay in place,
Will not stay still.[1]

Our speech must be clarified and also our understanding
of the meaning of what we say. It is the theologian's task to
clarify the church's talk about God. The linguistic analyst in
turn helps the theologian clarify his talk about God by asking
repeatedly, "What do you mean by that?" And all of this is
to the good, for density is not a virtue, even when practiced
by Christians. "If he is the Christ, tell us plainly."

It is in order that the church repent, but only up to a point.
For there is an important sense in which the world's craving
for clarity is a craving that we *should not* and *cannot* satisfy.
Should not, because the kind of clarity that Mr. Average Man
is seeking is what might be described as "computer clarity."
There is grim point to that computer joke in which a man
stands before this massive machine and asks, "Is there a God?"
The answer comes back, "There is now."

Computers are eminently helpful with questions of fact and
quantity. But what about questions that partake of mystery
because they deal with loyalties and relationships? The church
is always tempted to give easy answers to hard questions, to
succumb to the heresy of exactness. There are questions of the
heart that cannot be answered with the plainness of a TV
commercial. The Bible is not an almanac nor the minister an
answer man.

My friend over at the university was right when he said
that there are certain parts of life to which a man must respond as a poet. There is a dimension of depth and mystery
to life that we dare not compromise. What is a tear, for

example? Here it is, right from the latest unabridged dictionary: "A tear is a drop of the saline watery fluid continually
secreted by the lacrimal gland between the surface of the eye
and the eyelid, serving to moisten and lubricate these parts
and keep them clear of foreign particles." [2] This is a tear?

A while ago the pages of *Saturday Review* carried a question from a disturbed mother who wanted to know what she
should say to her preschool daughter who had asked, "Where
was I when you were a little girl?" Two answers came in.
One woman said, "I had a four-year-old boy who asked me
that and I told him the truth. Half of you was a little tiny egg
without a shell waiting in a very special place inside my body
all the time Mommy was a little girl. Then, when Mommy
became a lady, God helped my body to make a soft, warm
place for you to grow, and your father planted a little seed
that made your egg whole, and you grew." The other answer
was sent in by a teaching nun in Missouri. "Where was I
when you were a girl?" The answer is simple: "In the mind
of God." [3] Both answers have their place. But I suspect that
the second is truer to life because it guards the mystery. The
first is so factual that it obscures a deeper truth.

Moreover, we *cannot* because the gospel to which we are
committed is itself a mix of light and mystery. It is true that
St. Paul understands the gospel as the unveiling of a mystery.
He writes to the Ephesians, "For he has made known to us in
all wisdom and insight the mystery of his will, according to
his purpose which he set forth in Christ" (Eph. 1:9, RSV).
But this same apostle acknowledges in another place that we
see as through a glass darkly and know only in part. Hugh
Thompson Kerr, in his very helpful book *Mystery and Meaning in the Christian Faith*,[4] points out that at every stage of
Christian experience there is both meaning and mystery. It
is not the case that if I study hard enough and discipline my-

self sufficiently light will break and all mystery disappear. No, at every level of Christian experience there is both meaning and mystery.

Historically, the Roman Catholic church has tended to perpetuate the mystery and Protestants have tended to emphasize meaning. This is why we are so word-oriented in our Protestant tradition. We set out to explain it all. Isn't this basically what the word "obscene" means, to bare that which rightly should be hidden? In our zeal to declare the truth we must remember that words alone cannot do it all, because words tend to dissipate the very mystery in which we must participate.

Verbal exactness can be misleading. This is why we need to enlist the help of the poet, the dramatist, the artist, the musician, the dancer when we desire to communicate. When Robert Frost's brief poem "Stopping by Woods on a Snowy Evening" was analyzed by John Ciardi for two and a half long pages, people began writing in to ask that certain of Frost's images be defined. Frost, however, refused to be pinned down. He wished his readers to grapple with mystery themselves. This is why Lesslie Newbigin reminds us that "to see the whole truth of the situation you must read the fiction of our time as well as the scientific and technical journals. You must attend the theatre as well as the seminar. You must consult with the psychiatrist as well as the cyberneticians. When you do this it is clear that there is another side to the picture." [5]

Take for one example the mystery of good and evil. G. K. Chesterton wisely noted that "the troublesome thing about life is not that it is rational or irrational but that it is almost rational." Berdyaev said, "I should say that the problem of evil is a scandal to all monistic philosophy and so it is also to the traditional doctrine of Divine Providence." [6]

Job grappled with the problem of how God could be reconciled to evil in the world, but was never given an answer. He was simply taken to a place where the mystery no longer disturbed his faith. We Christians get into real trouble when we attempt to interpret somebody else's providence to him. We have a way of rushing in where angels fear to tread. We would do well to remember a line from the hymn:

> Blind unbelief is sure to err
> And scan his work in vain;
> God is his own interpreter,
> And he will make it plain.[7]

A friend of mine killed a German soldier head-on in World War II. In some ways as he tells it, it was an unnecessary killing; at least it was to him. The fact that the victim was an exceedingly youthful man burdened his conscience all the more. Presently he was given a Silver Star for his "achievement." But the Star hung heavy on his uniform and he sought counsel of three different chaplains. Admittedly distraught and beside himself, he walked into the office of the first chaplain, flung the Star down on the desk and said, "Here, justify this!" The chaplain's answer was simply, "Render unto Caesar the things that are Caesar's." My friend grabbed the Star and said, "To hell with Caesar!" He went into the quarters of the second chaplain and the answer there was "Onward Christian Soldiers." He took the Star and went off to the third who happened to be a Southern Baptist preacher. "Justify this." The chaplain broke down and cried. Then they wept together. Finally they prayed. The soldier's question called not for clarity but for empathy.

"If Thou art the Christ, tell us plainly." "If he is the Christ, tell us plainly." We work to clarify our words and meaning but we let the mystery stand. President Nathan Pusey of

Harvard has said, "It would seem to me that the finest fruit
of serious learning should be the ability to speak the word
God without reserve or embarrassment, certainly without
adolescent resentment; rather with some sense of communion,
with reverence and with joy." [8] Surely we can wish this for
ourselves and others.

Closing Prayer

O God, we thank thee alike for words of piercing
clarity that light our way, and for every inti-
mation of the mystery that over and around us
lies.

So monitor our speech that we may neither over-
state nor understate, misstate nor leave unstated
the truth that has made us free.

Through Jesus Christ our Lord.

Amen.

CHAPTER 6

More to Come

"Here and now, dear friends, we are God's children; what we shall be has not yet been disclosed."

1 John 3:2a, NEB

Seventy-five years ago Christian congregations in the Western world could be characterized by a general sense of guilt. Ten years ago those same congregations could be characterized by a general sense of doubt. Today the temperature has dropped still further. A minister now may presume, no matter where he preaches, that the congregation gathered before him is beset with a sense of discouragement.

Discouragement has many fathers. It enters our lives from a variety of sources. But I am convinced that the main cause of discouragement, whether personal or corporate, is the inability to believe in a future that we can reach. Ironically, the more idealistic one is the more susceptible he is to discouragement. Only those who have expected much can know the bitterness of hopes denied. This helps to explain why discouragement infiltrates the ranks of the people of God.

Discouragement does not spare the pulpit any more than the congregation. One verse in particular has given me a sorely needed lift in recent months. It penetrates our mood the way a key penetrates a lock. "Here and now, dear friends, we are God's children; what we shall be has not yet been disclosed."

There are two stout affirmations in these words of the Apostle John. I suggest that we take the second one first. "What we shall be has not yet been disclosed." Or, as the familiar King James Version has it, "It doth not yet appear what we shall be."

What this means for us is that we have a future. There is more to come! There always is! We are not simply playing out the string. God is not finished with us yet. We are his workmanship and he is still building.

In fact, in the perspective of the long run, we have hardly started. There are unrealized capacities to recognize and develop. There are stubborn sins and weaknesses to overcome. There is knowledge to receive. There is love to give and take. In our lucid times we know that these are ours to struggle with whatever the system, the age, or the social context in which we move. After we have fired off that telegram to Congress and written our letter to the editor; after we have painted our posters, attended our rallies, signed our petitions and marched and picketed and whatever else; when we come home and turn the lock for the night we must still ask ourselves in solitude, "What manner of man am I?"

The self to be, as I understand John, is hardly recognizable from the self that is. "What we shall be has not yet been disclosed."

Granted, there is an eschatological note here. The next verse hints the dawn of a new age and a better world. "We shall be like him because we shall see him as he is" (1 John 3:2b, NEB). But every theologian I have ever read has insisted that sanctification begins here when we believe, not there when we die. Some of the most impressive arguments for the Christian life can be found in the quiet witness of men and women who have been seasoned not only by age but by the inner working of the Holy Spirit. The more clearly we see the Master, the more nearly we resemble him.

Once we have known him, we can never be pre-Christian again. Whether we want our future or not he draws us forward to it. "The man whose sickness is called 'Jesus' can never be cured." [1] We have a future, says John, and it is good. It does not yet appear what any of us will be.

Because this is true of us as individual Christians, it follows that it has not yet been disclosed what the church will be, for the church is nothing more than believers in community.

The church is here as harbinger of the kingdom of God. The church is not the kingdom of God and is always in trouble when it assumes that it is. We are, as it were, a presampling of what the reign of God will look like when it comes. Many times we are a misleading sampling—which is why we pray our prayers of confession.

Someday the church will be phased out. It will work itself out of a job. We are told by John that in his vision of the new Jerusalem, the city of God come down from above, "there is no temple there" (Rev. 21:24).

But prior to that, the church has a lustrous future. Paul, who knew as well as any man how petty and mean and frustrating the church could be, declares that it is God's intention "to present the church to himself all glorious, with no stain or wrinkle or anything of the sort, but holy and without blemish" (Eph. 5:27, NEB). I don't know how the church will get there from where it is today, but that is God's business, not mine. Christ not only gave himself *for* the church, he gives himself *to* the church, so that increasingly the church in its corporate life might resemble his will and reflect his desires.

There is no assurance here that the church as we have known it, its organizational forms, its liturgical forms, its programmatic forms, will be conserved. But we do know that the church's future is insured, and that some day it will appear in the eyes of all to conform flawlessly to the will of the one who loves it and gave himself for it.

It also follows that because the church has a future, the world has a future, too. The only reason the church is here is for the world. The existence of the church presumes the existence of the world and the continuity of history. The church is not an end in itself. It is solely, only, exclusively here for the sake of the world. Instead of regarding the Holy Spirit as a private source of empowerment for us who are the "in people," we should recognize that "the Holy Spirit is the Almighty God himself, and his breath blows through all creation." [2]

Salvation can be attributed to an elective act of God, *but so can creation.* He chose to create so that the world might be.

I think it is time for more of us to get ourselves up into a high place to remind a staggering country and a reeling world that history has a future, and that because that future is in the hands of God it is good. The Scriptures do not describe this future with the analytical clarity of an IBM printout, but we can warm our hearts around these hints of the coming day. The Scriptures indicate that the time will come when man will be constructively related to his fellows. Micah predicted an era "when swords will be beaten into plowshares and spears into pruning hooks; a time when nation shall not lift up sword against nation, neither shall they learn war any more; but they shall sit every man under his vine and under his fig tree, and none shall make him afraid" (Mic. 4:3–4a).

The Scriptures also speak of a time when man and God shall live in harmony. "For the earth will be filled with the knowledge of the glory of God as the waters cover the sea" (Hab. 2:14). The Scriptures anticipate an improvement in man's relationship with nature, and peace between the various elements of the natural order. "The wolf also shall dwell with the lamb, and the leopard shall lie down with the kid; and the calf and the young lion and the fatling together; and a little child shall lead them" (Isa. 11:6).

Paul tells us in the eighth chapter of his Roman Letter that "the creation itself," not just the church, "will be set free from its bondage to decay and obtain the glorious liberty of the children of God" (Rom. 8:21, RSV). Earlier he says, "For the creation waits with eager longing for the revealing of the sons of God" (Rom. 8:19, RSV). We will return to that verse at the end of this chapter.

In the Lord's Prayer we pray that the will of God might be done on earth, even as it is in heaven. Surely our Lord would not have encouraged us to pray an impossible prayer. When we talk in the Apostle's Creed about the resurrection of the body, are we not saying symbolically that we believe in the triumph of man's corporeal and spiritual nature and the world of history in which he lives? It was this kind of thinking that prompted Hendrikus Berkhof to say, "The new heaven and the new earth will be the transfiguration of this world, such as the work of man will have contributed to constitute it. In this sense the history of civilization as that of the cosmos enters into the total compass of the history of salvation." [3]

Evil is real but evil is limited. Satan is on a leash and God can bring him in. The Almighty never lets an age be tempted beyond its ability to stand—except when he is readying a new age to succeed it.

If we know all of this, why are we so discouraged? I suggest that discouragement overtakes us because we become so obsessed with our *proximate* goals that we fail to see how provisional they are and how little they resemble God's *ultimate* will. For example, it is commonly assumed when one of our politicians, in supporting a piece of proposed legislation, declares that America should never be anything but number one that he has spoken axiomatically, that is, his assertion is beyond question. In the name of our desire to maintain the number one position we have generated interest in bombers, revised economic policy, subsidized transoceanic shipping, and a host of other things.

I take pride as an American in the fact that we are an able and productive nation. I also see it as belonging to my Christian commitment to be a responsible citizen of this republic. But I cannot believe, nor can any of us, when we think about it, that the number one status of the United States belongs necessarily to the final vision of history.

Or again, think of New York City—which some of us residents never stop doing. There is a proximate goal to which all of us who live and work here are committed; namely, that our city might recover the preeminence that it once enjoyed. But even as we pursue this goal we ought to bear in mind that it is not absolutely necessary to the final vision of history that New York regain the primacy it once held.

One reason we became the greatest city in the world is because our commodious harbor was a boon to shipping. With shipping now on the decline, how important is the harbor today? One cannot book passage on an American liner for a trip to Europe, that's how important it is! The airplane has superseded the ship.

We used to be heavy on manufacturing in this city, but now the move is away from production to services. Manufacturers, for a variety of reasons, have found it profitable to go somewhere else. It was once necessary for large corporations to locate their main offices close to one another to facilitate communication. Now that we live post-telephone and post-teletype it is no longer necessary for corporate headquarters to be centered in a few key places.

We must be realistic about the future of our city and take into account factors that go beyond the sincerity and commitment of its citizens. There are demographical and economic aspects to consider. The final vision of the kingdom of God is not necessarily tied to the greatness of this or any other city!

Meanwhile, we work as if the future we envision were possible. In good faith, righting wrongs, easing burdens, encouraging the good. It is better to fail at the high altitude of noble resolution than to acquiesce abjectly in the city's attrition.

It may be said of this city that what it shall be has not yet been disclosed. What the city will be, what the world will be, what the church will be, or even what we will be individually does not yet appear. All we know is that a future divinely wrought keeps pulling us forward.

But how do we know that all of this is not, in Sigmund Freud's disparaging language, "a subjectively generated illusion?" How do we know that we are not simply putting ourselves on? Well, that's where the first part of the verse comes in. "Here and now, dear friends, we are God's children." This is the grand fact. This is what anchors our hope.

John is ecstatic about this. "Behold what manner of love the father hath bestowed upon us, that we should be called the sons of God" (1 John 3:1). That word "behold" suggests astonishment and amazement. "What manner" literally means "of what country." Where in the world did such love come from? It's out of sight—that *we* should be called the children of God. Not that we call ourselves such, for that would be unstable and arrogant. The wonder is that he should call us his children. And since the ground cause is in him we never need worry about unqualifying ourselves for we never qualified in the first place.

This is the most important fact about any who believe in Christ: each of us is a child of God. It is more significant that we are sons of God than to be a son of Italy, or a son of Ireland, or a son of Africa! Now, in the thick of our unemployment and inflation; now in the depressing aftermath of Attica; now, in the midst of a city's struggle to retrieve its glory; now, as ecological battles open on a hundred different fronts, *we are God's children.* His Spirit bears witness with our spirits that this is so. As John goes on to say, "And so we are."

In this confidence, wrought by a present possession and realization, we dare to long for the future that God is bringing to us. I was talking during my vacation with a British-born minister, now a teacher on the West Coast, about what I wanted to share with my congregation on my first Sunday back. He pointed me to a strong word in Romans 8:19, where St. Paul talks about "waiting with eager longing for the revealing of the sons of God." The key word in Greek is *apokaradokia.* This gentleman and his wife were so taken by that word that they named a beloved cat after it. Before you censure these good people for minor irreverence hear the story out.

The animal in question was a marmalade colored Persian cat. It had a long neck that was usually stretched out to the full, and a nose that most of the time was pointed up in curiosity. Its body was ever poised to press into new and unknown places. And that's how Marmalade Apokaradokia got his name!

The word in the Greek means to watch with head erect or outstretched, to direct attention to anything, to wait for in suspense. It connotes constancy in expecting. Forget the cat. Forget the word if you must. But remember the posture. We are called to live on the stretch because there is more to come. There always is. Our role is to *wait* for it, and to *watch* for it, and to *work* for it. "Here and now, dear friends, we are God's children; and what we shall be has not yet been disclosed."

CHAPTER 7

A Tourist in Your Own Hometown

Last week in a brief post-Easter vacation I did what I wanted to do for a long time and became a tourist in my own hometown. I stayed in New York City, disengaged myself from most of my regular commitments and sought to enjoy the city as one might who had never been here before.

There were long walks on Riverside Drive and a leisurely gambol through the Sheep Meadow of Central Park; two trips to the movies to catch up on pictures long on my "must-see" list; a worship experience in the Cathedral of St. John the Divine; a visit to the Aquarium at Coney Island, and time on the beach for the first baseball catch of the season; a hockey play-off game at Madison Square Garden; three well-spent hours at the Metropolitan Museum of Art; a walk through Chinatown, and the chance to be the only English-speaking party in a crowded Chinese restaurant at four in the afternoon. The only letdown came when we ordered tea and expected something exotic, only to find ourselves, minutes later, pressing a Tetley tea bag in a cup of boiling water.

I share these notes not to be unduly personal, but to launch us into a consideration of the importance of enjoying what we have where we are. "Tourists in Our Own Home Town." Why not?

It doesn't take a preacher to point out that a melancholia bordering on the pathological hangs over New York City like a poison-ridden fog. I would be the first to concede that Fun City is beset with a terrifying array of problems. We are short on money and long on the need for better social and protective services. Our transportation networks are suffering from poor circulation and hardening of the arteries. Pushers and addicts make us wince. Our schools are bulging and fast becoming ungovernable. Pride in the cleanliness of the city is at low ebb. Strikes and rumors of strikes make us alternately angry and inconvenienced. Rising costs coupled with shrinking dollars turn shopping into a nightmare for many families in our city.

In such a time it belongs to our sanity, not to mention our faith, that we enjoy the compensations that the city affords. To enjoy them even as we attack the problems. After all, there are tremendous demands for housing in New York City. Apparently thousands of people wish to live here. Our hotels and motels run full frequently. Apparently people by the thousands wish to come here. Why then do we tend to be indifferent to the treasures of the city? Why do we determine simply to endure the city in anticipation of a one-, two- or three-week period of vacation when we can go elsewhere to enjoy the earth?

To capture the tourist stance at least two things are required of us. The first is an aroused awareness of the sights

that lie around us, an eye for observation that will permit us to
see not in broad uninteresting generalities but in fineness of
detail. Gustave Flaubert said one time to his writing disciple
Henri de Maupassant: "You go down to the station and you
will find there about fifty cabs. They all look pretty much
alike, but they are not alike. You pick out one and describe
it so accurately that when it goes past I cannot possibly
mistake it."

"To be seeing the world made new every morning, as if it
were the morning of the first day, and then to make the most
of it for the individual soul as if each were the last day—is the
daily curriculum of the mind's desire," observed John Finley.[1]
We New Yorkers tend to concentrate so much on the immediate hustle in which we find ourselves that we do not
allow the history that lies behind our city to speak to us and
illumine our present experience. Annette Wynne's poem "Indian Children," known to many children, speaks to the way in
which history is always trying to break through to thicken our
experience of the present:

> Where we walk to school each day
> Indian children used to play,
> All about our native land,
> Where the shops and houses stand.
>
> And the trees were very tall,
> And there were no streets at all,
> Not a church, not a steeple—
> Only woods and Indian people.
>
> Only wigwams on the ground
> And at night bears prowling round—
> What a different place today
> Where we live and work and play! [2]

Along with this we need what I think most every tourist
to our city has, a fascination for the people of the city. The

people of New York are by far the most interesting part of New York. Perhaps it's because there are so many "characters" like us in the city. Have you ever noticed how frequently it is said of Jesus that he beheld the people who came before him? Individuals whom others would have passed off as part of the masses registered on his consciousness and he enjoyed them.

The pity is that we tend to see people only in terms of their functional value in our society. Joseph Haroutunian, who gave most of his latter years to an understanding of Christian community, has noted that "it becomes a habit to look at another man not as a fellowman but according to his function and power in Society—so much so that thinking men see the person as the sum of the roles he plays in the cluster of institutions in the city. Men are known as businessmen, government men, doctors, teachers, 'working men,' and so forth, first, and as fellowmen secondly; and this means that it is their power and not their fellowmanhood that impresses those who have communication with them." [3] Why not tell the newsman that you missed him when he was sick those four days! The mail carrier was a man before he ever toted a letter. How about inquiring of the pharmacist about his son away at school?

Let us be aware along with the pressures that we feel in the normal round of our life in this metropolis that there are also opportunities to revive and deepen life. Let's ask God to help us shed the blasé spirit of the stereotype New Yorker so that we might enjoy our home even as the tourist does.

> The spring blew trumpets of color,
>   Her green sang in my brain;
> I heard a blind man groping
>   tap-tap with his cane.

> I pitied him his blindness
> but can I say I see?
> Perhaps there walks close by a
> spirit that pities me.
>
> A spirit that sees me tapping the
> five-sensed cane of time;
> Amid such unguess'd glories
> that I am worse than blind! [4]

We need a similar enhancement of expectation and excitement in our experience of God. If ever the old adage holds that "familiarity breeds contempt," it surely holds in the realm of what man calls religion. How we Christians fail to prize and enter into our inheritance! We have been at it for such a long time, most of us—some of us as professionals pushing around words about the faith. Our zeal is in decline. We troop off after this minor cause and that, but somehow our hearts are not enkindled with any seeable enthusiasm. In the words of Scripture, it may be true of us that we have "lost our first love," that we are neither "hot nor cold," thus becoming dull to ourselves and a bore to those outside.

Perhaps part of the problem is that we came by our faith without struggle. The Catholic layman Michael Novak confesses: "I have often felt despair because God came to me too easily, before I had a chance, entering my blood and bones through my mother's milk. It might have been easier to decide freely whether to believe or to disbelieve if I had been born an atheist." [5] Graham Greene speaks the same way about the whiskey priest in *The Power and the Glory:* "The good things of life had come to him too early—the respect of his contemporaries, a safe livelihood. The trite religious word upon the tongue, the joke to ease the way, the ready acceptance of other people's homage . . . a happy man." [6]

How can we recover what we've lost? Kierkegaard asked it for us all when he said, "How can one who is a Christian become a Christian?" That is, how can one who is nominally tied to the establishment recover the ardor that rightly belongs to those who live unto Jesus Christ? Nicodemus asked, "How can a man be born when he is old?" (John 3:4a), in part, I'm sure, meaning, "How can one repossess the wondering eye of the child?"

Just as the tourist can perk up the zeal of the native so the convert can alert the veteran Christian to the value of his faith. I have in my files the story of a great sea painter who was searching for a boy in whose face he might find the wonder of the sea. He chose not a boy from the seacoast to whom the sea was nothing unusual, but a boy from the London slums who had never seen the ocean!

It would make an interesting study to consider what men and women wrote and said and felt who stumbled onto the Christian faith late in life, who approached the gospel with what might be called the "dimension of novelty." Thomas Carlyle, for example, said: "The older I grow—and now I stand on the brink of eternity—the more comes back to me the first sentence in the Catechism which I learned when a child, and the fuller and deeper its meaning becomes: 'What is the chief end of man? To glorify God and to enjoy him forever.' " [7]

Read again the autobiography of C. S. Lewis, *Surprised by Joy,* and you will find that Lewis, like so many others, found himself overtaken by the magnitude of Jesus Christ. Not the organization of the church. Not its programs which are here successful and there failures. Certainly not the ordered correlation of dogma in the form of theological propositions. But the magnificent, haunting presence of Jesus Christ overtook him. P. T. Forsyth was right: "Our real and destined eternity goes around by Nazareth to reach us. What abides in history is not the impression He made, nor a Church's report. But it is His historic self, prophetic and priestly still in the kingly way of eternity. He is born again in each soul that is born anew." [8]

Some of us may have been reading recently about Malcolm Muggeridge's rediscovery of Jesus. Here is a man in the latter part of life, a well-known editor in England who has served with distinction on *The Manchester Guardian, Punch,* and other well-known periodicals. This gifted writer was sent on a routine trip to Israel by the BBC in conjunction with a proposed telecast on the life of Jesus. He recalls in his moving book how in the midst of performing his professional duty it suddenly struck him that this One about whom the program would center was truly alive. Muggeridge writes: "Yet behind all this there is a real man—born, growing up, reaching maturity like other men; turning his mind, as I have tried to turn mine, to what life means rather than to what it provides; trudging through this self-same dust, and sheltering from this self-same sun; lying down at night to sleep, and rising in the morning to live another day." [9] Later on he says: "Not even a sparrow, we are told, can fall to the ground without causing God concern; all the material universe is, as it were, a message in code from God, which mystics, artists, and scientists strive to crack, sometimes with a measure of success, but to which Christ provides the key." [10]

Why not such adulation of the Christ? Why are we who know so well the gospel story so unable to be moved by his presence and his power? After all, he has kindled more fires of affection, induced more liberality, elicited more faith in God, encouraged and effected more reconciliation, inspired more art, set in motion more song and poetry than any other man that ever lived!

And the encouraging thought is that our ardor need not wane. Martin Luther was confronted with the opportunity of explaining to the newly emerging Protestant communities the meaning of Ascension. He said: "Therefore, beware lest you imagine within yourself that he has gone, and now is, far away from us. The very opposite is true: while he was on earth, he was far away from us; now he is very near." [11]

Evelyn Underhill has at times found me with her unnerving observation that there are those in the church who have deserted Christ and entered His service instead. We may be veteran members of the church, officers of the congregation, ministers of the Christian gospel, members of boards and agencies of the several denominations, distraught parents, or just plain cynical young people. Whoever we are, we must concede the presumption that if Jesus Christ is not thrilling us to the core of our being, the fault is not in him but in ourselves.

> Whoso draws nigh to God
>   one step through doubtings dim,
> God will advance a mile
>   in blazing light to Him.

Let me close with a slice of dialogue from George Bernard Shaw's *Saint Joan*. The archbishop, stirred by her composure and faith, says to Joan: "How do you know you are right?"

Joan replies: "I always know. My voices—."

King Charles retorts: "Oh, your voices, your voices. Why don't the voices come to me? I am king, not you."

Joan responds softly, "They do come to you; but you do not hear them. When the Angelus rings you cross yourself and have done with it; but if you prayed from your heart, and listened to the thrilling bells in the air after they stop ringing you would hear the voices as well as I do." [12]

To enjoy New York in the manner of a tourist, to celebrate our faith in the manner of a convert, this is our hope.

Closing Prayer

God, bless us, we pray thee, with the
    gift of awareness.
        To have eyes—and see,
        to have ears—and hear,
        to have the gift of touch—and feel,
        this we would know.
Bring to brighter flame our love for thee
    that it may make us both radiant
    and constant in thy service.
        Through Jesus Christ our Lord.
                    Amen.

CHAPTER 8

Inevitability and Responsibility

The Son of Man is going the way appointed for him in the
scriptures; but alas for that man by whom the Son of Man is
betrayed!

Matthew 26:24, NEB

The man said he was looking for a one-armed lawyer. "A
one-armed lawyer?" asked his friend. "How come?" The reply
came quickly, "I am looking for an attorney who won't say
'on the other hand, on the other hand.' "

Unfortunately, some truths require two hands. Philosophers
call such truths paradoxes. A paradox consists of two state-
ments about reality that appear to contradict one another,
neither of which is complete without the other.

We have a paradox in the text for this chapter. The words
come from Jesus' lips in the Upper Room as he comments
solemnly on Judas' intention to betray him. They are found
in Matthew 26:24, and in similar form in Mark and Luke.
"The Son of Man is going the way appointed for him in the
scriptures; but alas for that man by whom the Son of Man
is betrayed!"

The paradox here is obvious. On the one hand, what Judas was to do would be in fulfillment of a divinely conceived plan. "The Son of Man is going the way appointed for him in the scriptures." On the other hand, Judas will suffer for his deed: "but alas for that man by whom the Son of Man is betrayed!"

The Scriptures in several places suggest the inevitability of Jesus' being handed over to the authorities. For example, on the Emmaus Road the incognito Christ speaks to his fellow travelers and asks, "O foolish men, and slow of heart to believe all that the prophets have spoken! Was it not necessary that the Christ should suffer these things and enter into his glory?" (Luke 24:25–26, RSV). Or again, on the day of Pentecost after the Spirit came, Peter preached: "This Jesus, delivered up according to the definite plan and foreknowledge of God, you crucified and killed by the hands of lawless men" (Acts 2:23, RSV).

But, just as surely, the Scriptures suggest that Judas is responsible. Indeed, Judas testifies to his responsibility by his remorse, by his attempt to throw back the thirty pieces of silver, and most especially by his self-inflicted violent death.

What a mystery it all is! The disciple who betrayed his Lord was acting out a part. But the disciple who betrayed his Lord was called upon to bear punishment for his deed. If an action is inevitable, how can one be responsible for it? And if one is responsible for an action, how can it be said to be inevitable?

This paradox is not limited to Judas or the Scriptures. It appears time and again in formal thought and daily life. It is a constantly recurring theme in philosophy, where it is generally treated under the heading Determinism and Free Will. It intrudes into every psychologist's counseling room and every psychiatric consultation. It figures in the approach of the social worker as she makes her rounds and conducts her interviews. It influences the teacher's attitude toward her boys and girls.

It is more basic to the guidance counselor's office than desk or chairs or rug. It looms large in the minds of legislators, state and national, as they prepare to vote on social issues. Indeed, it has much to do with how a congregation understands its mission to the world. Are people responsible for their lives, or is some inevitability at work making us what we are?

Where a paradox exists, only the foolhardy would dare to resolve the matter by eliminating one of the propositions. Thus, in the course of history, not many have been willing to defend total determinism, or total freedom. The wise prefer to hold to a both/and, and to see life as a mix of the two. But the proportion of that mix has varied sharply from time to time and man to man. What is the actual situation? Is it three parts determinism and one part freedom? Is it fifty-fifty? What is it?

It seems to me that we are in deep trouble in our society today because we hold to a one-tenth, nine-tenths mix. We tend to believe or assume that life is nine-tenths inevitability and only one-tenth responsibility. Consider the mounting interest in astrology and horoscopes. Do the stars, in fact, *compel* us, or do they at most *impel?*

Consider the way people both old and young blame the system for their failings. We might very well paraphrase Shakespeare's famous lines and say, "The fault, dear Brutus, is not in ourselves, but in our structures that we are underlings."

But hasn't the system to which we ascribe such blame achieved power over us with our complicity, if not our direct consent? Can we in good faith borrow from Tin Pan Alley of another day and say to these systems—political, economic, and social—you made me love you, but I didn't want to do it? Haven't we at heart really wanted what the system had to offer? Have we not been eager to pay the price for what the system might bestow?

Henry Drummond, a character in Lawrence and Lee's dramatization of the Scopes Monkey Trial of 1926, *Inherit the Wind,* gives a pointed accounting of the cost of change. "Gentlemen," he says, "progress has never been a bargain. You've got to pay for it. Sometimes I think there's a man behind the counter who says, 'All right, you have a telephone; but you'll have to give up privacy, the charm of distance. Madam, you may vote; but at a price; you lose the right to retreat behind a powder puff or a petticoat. Mister, you may conquer the air; but the birds will lose their wonder, and the clouds will smell of gasoline.' " [1]

The system that we claim cramps freedom and stifles life is neither inevitable nor unalterable. It was made by man and can be changed by man. Years ago Alexis de Tocqueville said: "I am tempted to believe that what we call necessary institutions are often no more than institutions to which we have grown accustomed. In matters of social constitution the field of possibilities is much more extensive than men living in their various societies are ready to imagine." [2]

Consider the way in which we trace our personal failures to every door but our own. We tend to see ourselves as altogether caused or conditioned. By our glands and genes—à la behaviorism. By heredity factors. "What can you expect of me? Look at the parents I had." I stand with George Buttrick when he warns: "You and I have little right to blame our ancestry for sins which we commit against our posterity." [3]

Caused and conditioned by a demeaning environment. But can any man, *any man,* be completely controlled from without? And what of those, and their names are legion, who came out of poverty and did not find it necessary to surrender either their virtue or their faith. What of them?

Sympathy for the underdog is one of the hallmarks of American life. It is also a basic Christian disposition. *But that sympathy is misdirected and misapplied when it prompts us to excuse ourselves or others on the grounds of some spurious doctrine of inevitability.*

We need to be chastened by James's familiar word: "Let no one say [whether in poverty or affluence] when he is tempted, 'I am tempted by God'; for God cannot be tempted with evil, and he himself tempts no one; but each person is tempted when he is lured and enticed by his own desire" (James 1:13–14, RSV).

Some time ago a good friend of mine, a black minister, was discussing the drug problem in New York and a program that might begin to get at it in some small way. In the course of his presentation, this likable and knowledgeable brother said to a mixed assembly, "You white men will have to know that as far as drugs go we are totally puritanical. You in your writings and sermons may take a liberal line on the use of drugs, but we are convinced that for *our* people total abstinence is the only approach possible." It was refreshing to hear a man appeal to inner controls, challenge the power of the will, and ask people to stand up to life.

Consider, finally, in this connection, the feeling that has virtually paralyzed our city that ominous forces sweep over us that we cannot control, the ghastly sense that nothing can be done, the fear that we can't answer back to conditions of dirt and corruption, overcrowding and traffic congestion, foul air, and polluted waters. Can it be that we have forgotten what a metropolis can do and be when its people have a mind to work?

Let the new Trade Center nearing completion downtown

remind us of what can be done when our genius, our money management, and our public relations all converge on one particular site. If as a city we can raise those twin towers in tribute to the importance of international trade, by God we can build some housing for people as well, if we have the will to work! It it totally un-Christian to suspect that we are under some nemesis-like fatality. It is not a fatality that we are up against, it is our own inertia!

It has been widely and wisely noted that in our time the critical question is whether we can give as much attention to collective survival as we formerly gave to individual survival. The fact of the matter is that if we don't begin to give a damn for something besides Number One, that number will be reduced to an inconsequential zero. Aristophanes in *The Frogs* has Euripides say: "I hate the citizen who, by nature well endowed, is slow to help his city, swift to do her harm, to himself useful, useless to the community." [4]

"The Son of Man is going the way appointed for him in the scriptures; but alas for that man by whom the Son of Man is betrayed!" Inevitability and responsibility are parts of every life. Rollo May writes in his helpful book *Love and Will:* "And though it is arrogance to say we are the 'masters of our fate,' we are saved from the need to be the victims of it. We are indeed co-creators of our fate." [5] This is good psychology and even better theology.

Robert Valentine once compared Teddy Roosevelt and William Howard Taft as presidents. He said, "The difference was that when you left Teddy Roosevelt's presence you were ready to eat bricks for lunch, and when you left Taft you felt—what's the use."

No one in history ever had a stronger sense of living out a divine design than Jesus. Yet, Jesus found it possible, knowing that design, to be constantly busy about his father's business. Men left his presence changed and prepared to change the world. Men still leave his presence convinced that they can work together with God in the world.

Inevitability and responsibility. The mystery will doubtless remain unresolved for us to death and beyond. Nevertheless, let us not blame our stars, or our systems, or our genes, or our parents, or our surroundings for what a strong faith and radical obedience to Christ could change!

Closing Prayer

God, we are well aware that life acts on us.
Make us at least equally aware that we act
  on life.
Get us off our heels and on our toes.
Away from the wailing wall and into the
  mood to build according to the vision
  of a world at peace with itself and thee.
Amen.

CHAPTER 9

Humane but Not Naive

In the early hours of the morning a shot rings out in an almost deserted subway car. At the next stop three teenagers bolt through the doors, rush to the street, and lose themselves in the night. Even as they run, a slumped body is discovered in that train. A man in his sixties has been shot through the heart and robbed. His life is over.

Within hours—through press, radio and television—the city is made aware that another heinous crime has been committed. Nearly everyone reacts—aloud or to himself. The responses reduce to two. Some say, "They ought to catch those kids and put them away for life!" Others lament the crime but wonder aloud how those young men got that way and how they might be helped.

To apply loose-fitting labels to these positions one would call the first conservative and the second liberal. Hard and soft might be a better way of distinguishing between them. Hard or soft, conservative or liberal, brand them how you will—which response comes closest to being Christian?

The man who wants to see the perpetrators caught and put away is entitled to be heard. Crime is a menace to society and a threat to liberty. As the late Justice Cardoza observed, "Men must find repose in the peace of the state."

The man of conservative temperament is grieved that so many intellectuals have gone too far in making allowances for criminal behavior: loveless homes, tough neighborhoods, racial discrimination, inferior schools, subhuman housing, the war in Vietnam.

This man wonders why the principle of extenuating circumstances is selectively applied. Why don't we, on the same grounds, excuse the heroin pusher, the slumlord, the excessively physical cop or the short-sighted warden? If we keep on excusing men their crimes what will become of personal responsibility and accountability? Where will it all end?

There is a scene in the novel *All Quiet on the Western Front* that in a way is a parable for our time. Soldiers in a hospital become annoyed by the singing outside their room, and one of them throws a bottle through the door to put a stop to the noise. When the inspector comes in to investigate, one of the soldiers confesses, even though it is apparent to all that he was not guilty. The inspector takes his name, turns on his heel without a word, and departs. The others ask, "But why did you say you did it? It wasn't you at all." He grins and answers, "That doesn't matter. I got a crack in the head and they presented me with a certificate to say that I was periodically not responsible for my actions. Ever since then I've had a grand time!" [1]

The man who wants strict law enforcement is disturbed about a society that weeps for the criminal and forgets the victim. Prisoners have a collective identity and visibility. They are a recognized and distinguishable segment of society. Victims of crimes, on the other hand, are fragmented and unorganized. Thus, they are void of power and their side of things tends to be underpresented.

Most importantly, this man whom we are trying to portray fairly is convinced that justice belongs to his faith. As far back as Plato and on through Aristotle and others, we have learned to think of justice as having two dimensions. Distributive justice gives to any his due. Retributive justice, which is the same in negative terms, stands for the deprivation of goods or active punishment. The man of faith yearns to see wrongs redressed and imbalances made right because he feels that justice is of God.

He is not at all sure that those passages in the Old Testament that deal with the administration of justice can be dismissed as so much outgrown counsel. The word from the Book of Deuteronomy, the familiar *lex talionis,* is a case in point. Actually, this was not an encouragement to vengeance. It was really an attempt to curb excessive vengefulness. An eye, yes, but only for an eye; not an eye for a finger. A tooth, yes, for a tooth; not a tooth for a finger. A life, yes, but only for a life; not for anything less.

The conservative Christian citizen will not buy any theory of rehabilitation that lacks the retributive dimension. He does not wish to be naïve.

But the man who wonders how the criminal got that way and how he might be helped must have his innings too. This type of individual is terribly troubled that society seems to be more concerned about the vices to which the poor succumb than about the social evils from which they suffer. He is aware of the correlation between crime and poverty. The unemployment rate in this country right now, for example, is twice as high for blacks as it is for whites. Eighty percent of black crimes committed in this country have to do with money, usually with very small amounts.

Moreover, the man who is concerned for the criminal believes that a sharp upturn in the crime rate can be traced in large measure to the general unrest and disease that mark the social order.

Plato long ago said, "It is useless to try by endless reform to cure rascality in a state when its fundamental order is wrong." [2] George Jackson makes the same point in his prison letters: "When the peasant revolts, the student demonstrates, the slum dweller riots, the robber robs, he is reacting to a feeling of insecurity, a reaction to the fact that he has lost control of the circumstances surrounding his life." [3]

The man who is concerned about the perpetrator of crime suspects that the judicial system discriminates against the little people. A gentleman whom I know, an executive of a reputable corporation in western Pennsylvania, told me not long ago about an incident in which his son was involved that eventually issued in the son's arrest. This was a "first" for this middle-class family. As a father he wondered what to do. The son was being held for ten thousand dollars bail, subsequently reduced to four thousand. My friend called his attorney and discovered that because he owned property he could have his son released immediately on a real estate bond. This was done, and all for a modest outlay of six dollars. Said the man, "I realized for the first time that one who is propertied in our society gets an early break in the judicial process."

Eighty-five percent of the prisoners in New York State's jails are black or Puerto Rican. We are not to deduce from this, however, that blacks and Puerto Ricans are inherently more criminal. We might better begin to reckon with these factors: that the poor because they are poor have inferior legal defense; that they are driven by a hopelessness and despair which the rest of us do not know; that many of them, because of poverty, lack a united home, either because of divorce or because both parents must go out each day to work; that *their* crimes are more diligently detected and more vigorously prosecuted.

The man who wants to know how those youngsters got that way, and what might be done to help them, occasionally becomes cynical about justice and sees it as "a fine name for the interests of the stronger."

The conservative and the liberal, the hard and the soft—you guessed it. They are not really two different people at all, are they? They are the two voices that vie with each other inside every one of us. We all aspire towards being humane. We all wish not to be naïve. We are destined to live with this tension all our days.

We bring this tension with us to the matter of prison reform. On this lively and timely subject we do not wish to be naïve. I was taken by surprise when out with a group of people not too many weeks ago. One of them said, "We've got to get together and work hard to get rid of prisons in this country." From such sentimentality, good Lord, deliver us! Crime is real. Criminals are a threat to society. Society has a right to protect itself from the criminal. Sometimes I think our sentimental Christians would do well to ride a police car on a Saturday night to get a feel for what it's like to be present when the passions of men explode. Trying to save men from the fury of other men isn't like running a Sunday school class. Societies have always had their prisons, their cemeteries, and their altars. These are inescapable parts of any culture.

No good is to be served by seeking to make a hero out of the criminal. The interesting thing about this point is that most of the criminals with whom I have spoken do not wish to be lionized in that way. During Christmas week I visited the state prison at Stormville, N.Y., and had the pleasure of talking intimately with some twenty to twenty-five inmates. There wasn't a one that took me into a corner to tell me that he had been imprisoned falsely. One man, I think, spoke the mood of all when he said, "It wasn't my mother or father. It wasn't my teachers. I made a damn fool out of myself and I am trying hard to see that my son doesn't make the same mistake." This is what Hegel meant when he said, "The criminal has a right to punishment." [4]

It is naïve to sentimentalize either crime or prisons in our society. One thinks of the judge who asked a defendant whom he had just sentenced if he had anything to say. The man replied, "Yes, your honor, let bygones be bygones."

I do not believe that our basic temptation today is to be naïve. Our overriding temptation is to fail to be humane.

Often one hears people say that we are doing too much to coddle the prisoner. Many on the outside resent giving the prisoner any amenities at all. The feeling persists that the more we can deprive the inmates, the more effectively justice is being served.

Over the years I have visited not only in Green Haven, but in Sing Sing and in county jails in the South, in Pennsylvania and in Michigan. I share with you the conviction that it is penalty enough to put a man behind bars; to shut him out from life; to shut him off from family; to shut him in with criminal types. There is nothing that we need add to that dispiriting experience to further the cause of justice.

At the present time it may well be that the best action a Christian church could take would be to confess that we have gone along with a basically inhumane system, and stand contritely before God for correction. Prisoners have suffered from our neglect. The prisoner out of sight is soon out of mind. We have not been concerned to learn what goes on in his world day by day. Like the good people of Gadara who took the demoniac and chained him outside the town so that they would not have to look on his form again, we have a way of shunting the prisoner off from our line of sight.

Moreover, we have subscribed, directly or indirectly, to a system that is predominantly custodial and only in the most minimal way remedial or rehabilitative. We call our institutions "correctional" facilities, but this is a myth and a laugh. Nationally we spend ninety-five percent of our prison budget for custody. These funds go to purchase iron bars, to build stone walls, to secure guards and guns. Only five percent of that national budget is spent on hope; that is, for health services, education, and the development of employment skills.

In New York City the current allocation looks like this: six hundred and fifty million dollars a year for police, one hundred million dollars for courts, and only sixty-five million dollars for correction. Is it any wonder we have had our prison riots and face the threat of more? Is it any wonder that the recidivism rate in this country is as high as eighty percent? We do so little for our prisoners when they are confined, and we are so inept on their behalf when they are released.

Commissioner Patrick Murphy, who keeps coming through as a man in public office who wants to do the right thing by all concerned, has said, "We do no more for the criminal in jail than we do for animals in the zoo. We cage them and feed them. The uglier and grimier and older the prison, the more it has seemed to the average citizen to be a fine and splendid prison." [5]

But it is good news to know that today there is a mood stirring in the land at large and surely within the church that we should be busy about making some corrections on our correctional institutions. Council VII (Riverside Church's Council on Social Relations) has created a task force expressly for this purpose. This task force will help us to understand the prisoner, and to relate to the ex-prisoner through the Fortune Society and a new and daring program known as The South Forty Corporation.

An experience is not an experience until you have experienced it. I would hope that, through the efforts of Council VII, prisoners would cease being mere statistics in our minds and start becoming real human beings. Personal contacts will surely bring this about. With the help of the grace of God let us get busy on their behalf.

Ramsey Clark points to society's stake in the penal system: "No activity of a people so exposes their humanity or inhumanity, their character, their capacity for charity in its most generous dimension, as the treatment they accord persons convicted of crime." [6] Our society is on trial in this matter and not the prisoner.

But the church has an even greater stake. If there is any gold at all in the current Black Theology it lies in the truth that God is always and unceasingly with the oppressed. The church is not at its best when it serves the interests of the respectable and the affluent. The church is at its best when it serves the hungry and the thirsty, the stranger and the naked, the sick and the imprisoned. Doing something for them, said Jesus, is like doing something for me!

Closing Prayer

Lay upon our hearts, O Lord,
　　the needs of those whom we would
　　　　prefer to forget—especially
　　the men and women in our
　　　　penal institutions.

Mindful of our frailties,
  make us generous toward theirs.
And show us how to serve thee,
  serving them.
    Through Jesus Christ Our Lord.
            Amen.

CHAPTER 10

The Seesaw View of Life

A. C. Spectorsky in his book The Exurbanites *offers this commentary on American manners:* "On the New York Central's commuting train down the Harlem Valley there are still seats aplenty at Chappaqua, and the courtly, old-world grace with which women are permitted to climb on board first would delight the most captious. By the time the train arrives at Pleasantville, however, seats are scarcer and only the most attractive or the most decrepit women are given any priority. Come White Plains and women are thrust aside; every man for himself." [1]

It's easy to be generous when there's enough to go around. But when supplies are limited this is quite a different matter. When there are three cars and only two parking places; five men wanting work and only four job openings; ten nations needing oil and only enough for nine. What then? It is in the crucible of scarcity that what we are and what we believe are most clearly revealed.

The specter of scarcity is beginning to impose its eerie presence on the American way of life. Ever since Pilgrim days we have lived with the notion that our frontiers and resources were perpetually expandable. Settlers who couldn't make it in the East pushed on across the Alleghenies. Those who could not find land to their liking in Kansas could rig up their wagons and roll on to Oklahoma. Those whose prospects for the good life were stymied in Ohio could cross the Rockies to pan for gold or dig for silver.

The prodigality of nature was consistently assumed. If a man needed a house he chopped down enough trees to build one. When he was hungry he shot a buffalo or deer. If he dug for copper and exhausted a particular mine he would simply snap a lock on the front gate, pack up his gear, and go digging somewhere else. We were still at Chappaqua. There was plenty of room for all!

As industrialization set in, however, we began to feel the pinch of want just a bit. Not having everything we needed, we used our wealth to trade for vital resources. Every year this country imports more than fifteen billion dollars' worth of goods—agricultural products, metals, and non-metallic minerals such as petroleum. The notion persisted that whether home-grown or imported we could get what we had to have. There was no reason other than mental stagnation or plain laziness why the Gross National Product could not go up, and up, and up each year! We were at Pleasantville now. Seats were not quite as plentiful as before, but if a man kept his wits and worked hard everything would be all right.

Now suddenly we are at White Plains, at the "every-man-for-himself" stage! The frontiers are gone, geographically speaking. Much of nature that we ravaged en route to our prosperity has been rendered permanently sterile. Old sources of vital foods and minerals are drying up. Countries that were once willing to trade away precious commodities to us are beginning to have second thoughts. Enormous pressures are being exerted on the United States by members of the Third World—Africans, Asians, South Americans, and impoverished blacks, whites, browns, reds, and yellows of our own country. More and more people are wondering why those of us in North America who comprise but 20 percent of the world's population should consume 80 percent of the world's wealth.

What is new in our situation is a growing awareness that we live in a finite universe. God is infinite, but the world is not. This has always been theoretically true, but now it is actually and existentially true. We live on a seesaw. If one is up too high, another must be down too low. Whether I intend it or not, my indulgence in luxury may deprive a brother of some necessity. Asking for seconds at the table is harmless enough—unless, of course, you know of a neighbor who hasn't eaten for three days, and especially if that neighbor's toil has helped to set your table!

This is what Adlai Stevenson was trying to lay on our hearts when he said: "We travel together, passengers in a little space ship all committed for our safety to its security and peace. We cannot maintain it half fortunate, half miserable, half confident, half despairing, half slave—to the ancient enemies of man—half free in a liberation of resources undreamed of until this day. No craft, no crew can travel safely with such vast contradictions. On their resolution depends the survival of us all."

What response can we make? What response should we make to all of this? Let me suggest some general and specific answers to that question. First, in a general way, we must

insist that the issues involved are moral as well as economic.
The balance of trade is in the picture. Import tariffs and
quotas are in the picture. The law of supply and demand is
in the picture. Hard money-soft money is in the picture. Inflation and deflation are in the picture. But these are not the
only factors in the situation. The World Bank is important
in all of this, but so is the world's conscience. We must not
sit back to enjoy our privileges on the assumption that in-
exorable economic law will have its way.

This is why Pope Paul VI in his encyclical *Populorum
Progressio* ("On the Development of Peoples") was moved
to say: "No one is justified in keeping for his exclusive use
what he does not need, when others lack necessities." [2]

Moreover, we must ease up on our habit of blaming the
poor for their poverty and crediting the affluent for their
wealth. You know how it goes—"He's where he is because
he's lazy and shiftless." "Modesty aside, I'm where I am because I'm good, and wise, and a hard worker." A professional
football coach told it like it is the other day when he noted
that the margin between a winning and losing team is very
slight. The bounce of a ball. The fracture of a bone. A
referee's decision.

In our better moments we know that the thinnest possible
line separates the destitute and the affluent, and that this line
was not of *our* making in the first place.

Moreover, still speaking generally, if we who stand in the
Hebrew-Christian tradition take our Scriptures seriously, we
must recognize that God's sympathies are unfailing and un-
alterably with the poor! Touch down where you will: Boaz
telling his young farmworkers not to pick the grain too clean,
Ruth needed some. Or the prophets telling the people in
several generations to make provision for the widow, the
orphan, and the stranger. Amos coming down hard on the

wealthy for the way in which they had taken or extorted unfair pledges from the poor. And the Apostle Paul in this
passage from Ephesians: "Let the thief no longer steal (here
all the law and order people say Amen), but rather let him
labor (those opposed to welfare say Amen), doing honest
work with his hands." But notice the purpose of our wealth:
"so that he may be able to give to those in need" (4:28,
RSV). That's what money is all about. And supremely, we
have that awesome "inasmuch" of Jesus: "Inasmuch as ye
have done it unto one of the least of these my brethren, ye
have done it unto me" (Matt. 25:40, KJV).

But to be more specific, let me suggest that there are some
assumptions or axioms that we Americans have been living
on that must be reconsidered. J. Irwin Miller, at one time
the layman president of the National Council of Churches,
once remarked that "history is full of tragedies of persons who
didn't understand the world in which they lived, and who
conducted their affairs as if in a world that had in fact been
long dead." [3]

I would suggest that we must reopen as citizens of this
country such assumptions as the unchecked expansion of
national economies, the right of everybody to have as large
a family as he wishes, the absolute value of human life over
all other life.

But coming closer to home, there is something we can do
as members of a given congregation. We can seek so to re-
order our investments that the social betterment of men,
rather than the highest monetary return, may govern what
we do. Most churches that I have known have been too much
oriented to Wall Street and too little oriented to the Jeru-
salem-Jericho road. We have been more concerned about the
Dow-Jones average than the Good Samaritan norm!

Even closer to home as individual members of our own

church, I believe that given the crisis of mounting scarcity it
is incumbent upon us that we consider a simpler style of life.
If some of our hippies have prodded us in this direction,
thank God for their witness.

A news item the other day released the word that corporations are having a hard time getting executives to come to
New York. It seems that New York City cannot provide them
with the "amenities to which they have grown accustomed."
This leads one to wonder what businessmen in France had
the coziest amenities before the Revolution.

It's so hard to come down once you have been up there.
I interceded once for a man who was store manager for a
nationwide chain. His salary was around the forty thousand
a year mark. He had been weighed in the balances by top
management and found wanting and was summarily fired.
When I got to the president of the company, I asked if my
parishioner might be given another store to manage. The
answer was, "No, he doesn't have it." Could he not then be
made a departmental manager in some other store? The
answer was, "No. We've learned that psychologically this
never works. Once you have been a manager you can't come
down."

Is there no power in the gospel? Is there no compulsion in
the mercy of God? Is there no illumination in the model of
Jesus himself that could make us willing to come down if
perchance it would help others to come up? Besides, does it
not belong to the wisdom of the gospel to give what we cannot keep to gain what we cannot lose?

I know of one denomination that has asked its members to
consider this covenant: "In view of our common responsibility in Christ to share with all men the life and resources
God has given us on the earth, I declare my intention to join
in the following covenant with others:

1. I will encourage business and appropriate levels of government to support opportunities for all people to participate in economic development.

2. I will involve myself in both study and action related to development of social justice and human dignity so that materially, socially, politically, and spiritually, we all may be free to be the responsible human beings God intended us to be.

3. I will contribute at least two per cent of my income annually for self-development of people in the world, including the United States of America. These contributions are to be a sign of my commitment and they are in addition to my normal gifts to church and community projects.

4. I will participate in confronting others personally with the idea of sharing in the self-development of people through a gift of two per cent over and beyond present giving."

The seesaw is in effect. We may not be comfortable with this, but this is a fact of life. When someone is up too high, someone else is down too low. But with love, the love of God for us—His love in us, there is no seesaw model. The beauty of God's love is that the more it is lavished, the more it grows; the more we act on it the more we have. It is to this love that I ultimately appeal. I believe our country can do it. I believe the church can do it. I believe that severally and individually as members of a congregation we can do it. And I believe we should.

Ministers who go to college campuses these days feel the resistance to the church and deep resentments toward the church that many young people harbor today. I wasn't helped on a recent trip to Indiana when the gentleman who led in the opening worship began with these words:

I was hungry
and you formed a humanities club
and discussed my hunger.
Thank you.

I was imprisoned
and you crept off quietly
to your chapel in the cellar
and prayed for my release.

I was naked
and in your mind
you debated the morality of my appearance.

I was sick
and you knelt and thanked God for your health.

I was homeless
and you left me alone
to pray.

You seem so holy,
so close to God
But I'm still hungry
and lonely
and cold.

So where have your prayers gone?
What have they done?
What does it profit a man
to page through his book of prayers
when the rest of the world
is crying for his help?

God speed the day when this indictment of the church will
be no longer true!

CHAPTER 11

Over Nature—Under God

Thou hast given him dominion over the works of thy hands;
thou hast put all things under his feet.

Psalm 8:6, RSV

It has been reliably established that different species of ani-
mals act as if they were members of the same family in the
face of common danger. Whether it be forest fire, flood or
drought, they face it not singly but as a group.

Earth Week with its assorted programs, speeches, and
demonstrations has heightened our awareness that we are on
a collision course with disaster unless we begin to restore
the gentle balances of nature.

It doesn't matter what our religious, political, social, cultural, or aesthetic "thing" may be. If our biosphere can no
longer sustain life, then all our causes will be indiscriminately
snuffed out. A common danger of the first magnitude is upon
us, and it remains to be seen whether humankind will be able
to close ranks in order to meet that danger.

If Christians are to play their part to the full in this emergency, they must look again to what they believe about man's relationship to the natural order. A serious charge has been leveled against the Judeo-Christian tradition on this very point by concerned scholars such as Lynn White and Roderick Nash of the University of California. It is their contention that the creation narratives in Genesis I and II have given man license to assault and exploit the universe. Because man sees himself as made in the image of God, and feels himself commissioned to subdue and have dominion over every living thing, he goes on to assume that the world is his oyster to do with as he wills. The implication is clear: we must get away from the Bible to get on with salvaging the earth!

What response can we make to this sobering charge? We could ask whether the biblical point of view was ever this influential—even in the Western world. I am inclined to agree with George Buttrick's contention in his book *God, Pain and Evil* that "the chaos of our world has come only in part from the failure of the church for the prevailing 'religion' ever since the Enlightenment has been humanism." [1]

We could cite men like John Muir, John Wesley Powell, and Clifford Pinchot, all celebrated conservationists, each of whom was identified with the Christian faith and active in the life of the church.

We could ask how critics of the biblical tradition account for the rape of nature in lands where the Bible has had little or no influence at all.

We could look more closely at the critical verbs in those Genesis passages with the hope that the lexicographer would help us to tone them down. Unfortunately, this hope must remain unrealized. The key words cannot be shorn of their terror and power. The Hebrew words involved are the verbs *kabash* and *radah*. They really do mean, based on use in other places, "to subdue, to bring into bondage, to rule over, to exercise dominion." *Kabash* has the thought of "stamping upon"—as when a man treads grapes with his feet. One "subdues" his enemies—they are placed under his feet. Israel subdued the land that she conquered. Both words have also been used to describe an owner's relationship to his slaves.

There is, I think, a more promising response that we could make. It would be in the form of a confession—a confession that in embracing the Genesis view of man, we have accentuated man's privileges and failed to reckon with man's responsibilities. True, man is, according to the Bible, over nature. He was given the privilege of naming every living thing, and power inheres in the one who gives the name. He was, indeed, commissioned to subdue the earth. He was directed to exercise dominion over every living thing. But just as man was made to be over nature, so was he also made to be under God. This is the all-important balancing fact that restores sanity to the picture.

One cannot read the creation accounts in Genesis I and II without sensing that the primary character, the first actor, the major figure is God, not man! Man's power is not absolute, it is derived. It is a conferred power, not an innate right.

The eighth Psalm, the only passage in Scripture that treats the image of God idea outside of Genesis, declares: "Thou hast given him dominion over the works of thy hands, thou hast put all things under his feet." The important thing here is to see that man's dominion has been given to him. It is God who has put all things under his feet. The same Bible that tells us about man's dominance over nature also affirms that "the earth is the Lord's, and the fulness thereof, the world and those who dwell therein" (Psalm 24:1, RSV).

When we go about the business of mutilating or exhausting nature as though we were all-powerful, nature has the right to say to us what Jesus said to Pilate: "You would have no

power over me unless it had been given you from above"
(John 19:11, RSV).

Gerhard von Rad, the distinguished Old Testament scholar,
puts it this way: "Just as powerful earthly kings, to indicate
their claim to dominion, erect an image of themselves in the
provinces of their empire where they do not personally appear, so man is placed upon the earth in God's image as
God's sovereign emblem." [2]

We are stand-ins for God vis-à-vis the natural order. More
than a mere reverence for life, we need a solicitude for life.
It may have been true in times past that man had to prove
his *machismo* by overmastering nature—as when the Hebrews
conquered their promised land, as when our forefathers on this
continent beat back the wilderness. But the need to demon-
strate such *machismo* is over. Nature requires of us now not
cruel domination, but tender, loving care.

When Robert Louis Stevenson was thirty-one, he came
upon a man one day in Pitlochry who was beating his dog.
Stevenson, always a great lover of nature, interposed himself
between the man and the dog. The owner objected. "It's not
your dog," he cried. But Stevenson answered, "It's God's
dog, and I'm here to protect it." Over nature, yes! But also
under God!

If we believe that this is man's authentic relationship to
the natural order, what can we do in the present crisis?
Fortunately, there is something that each of us can do. Let
me suggest a few possibilities. First, we can help to clean
things up where we are. I watched a man one morning
over on Broadway trying to sweep up the remnants of the
night. Paper, boxes, and leaves were scurrying everywhere at
the touch of the wind. Drawing near, I said, "You know, it
really doesn't matter much what you do. This wind keeps
whipping up more." But he would not be dissuaded. He answered simply, "I always get what I see."

Can you imagine the difference that would be evident in our several towns and cities if each of us "got what we saw," if we were attentive as Christian citizens about the way we package our garbage, walk our dogs, and make use of the litter basket.

Jerome Kretchmer, New York City's Environmental Protection Commissioner, astutely observed that "the litter basket is the first line of defense in the battle against litter. It is a tangible invitation to the individual to join in the job of creating a cleaner city." [3]

We can begin where we are to encourage the various entrepreneurs with whom we deal in the direction of cleanliness —rebuking them graciously when their premises or walkways are dirty and congratulating them when things are tidy and neat.

Beyond this, we can support with increased vigor those men and women in Congress who are sensitive to environmental issues. To my mind nothing more heartening has come out of the present Congress than the defeat of the SST. This triumph holds out hope that a new set of values is coming to birth in the life of our country. If history takes us to the point where we have to choose between good ecology and bad business, let our leaders know that every time we are in favor of good ecology.

Long before the bulldozer, Henry David Thoreau said: "If a man walks in the woods for love of them half of each day, he is in danger of being regarded as a loafer; but if he spends his whole day as a speculator, shearing off those woods and making earth bald before her time, he is esteemed an industrious and enterprising citizen. As if a town had no interests in its forests but to cut them down." [4]

We also have the power to bring some influence to bear on large corporations. If we are part-owners of these corporations, by virtue of the shares we hold, does it not belong to our citizenship and our Christian understanding of life to let management know that we would be willing to do with a smaller return in the interest of an improved environment? There is something manifestly unfair about pressing those corporations for maximum profit, while at the same time professing a keen concern for an improved environment.

As consumers of the products of these corporations we have the power to publicly resent and reject those goods that are produced with built-in obsolescence. We can cast the vote of our dollars for those products and containers that will bring us nearer the kind of world we would wish for ourselves and for our children.

The younger couples of us can play their part by resolving to limit their families to two children. It is very disturbing to reckon with the fact that even though we are only 6 percent of the world's population, we Americans consume 50 percent of the world's nonrenewable resources. If the current population growth persists, in thirty years we will constitute 4.5 percent of humanity, but will be using 80 percent of the world's nonrenewable resources.

Peter A. Jordan, Assistant Professor of Wildlife Ecology at Yale University, has commented on the importance of Americans limiting their families. His argument is based on the fact that we tend to consume so much more of the nonrenewable assets of the world than other people. He says, compellingly: "Although our rate of one percent increase per annum is well below the world's frightening 2.5 percent, each increment of our growth has manyfold times more impact upon diminishing resources and space and environmental quality than increments anywhere else on earth. Each one of us demands and uses up so much more of things physical and biotic, that one extra American has the ecological impact of 10, 20, or 100 extra Asians or Africans." [5] Does it not belong to our Christian citizenship to consider seriously the ethic of the two-child family?

Over nature, yes! But also under God. We have been called to participate in this wonderful thing called "being alive." We are commissioned to work with God and with each other to help make room for tomorrow! As we move in a matter of minutes to the bread and the cup let us be reminded that the life of grace is dependent on the fruits of nature. For it wasn't just us whom God loved. God so loved the *world*. *All* of nature awaits with us the day of full redemption!

CHAPTER 12

Overheard at Thirty Thousand Feet

Harry Watson was a clergyman in his late thirties. He thought of himself as young and vigorous even though his hair was thinning some and his midriff showed the effects of too many meat loaf suppers and chicken dinners. Fourteen years ago, Harry had won a prize in New Testament upon graduating from seminary. His work now as a chaplain at a Midwestern university made him more an activist than a scholar.

In fact, he was just now returning home from Washington, D.C., on a Friday evening flight in order to keep a Sunday speaking engagement. He had brought a busload of students to the nation's capital for two days of marching and rallying on behalf of the Welfare Rights movement. He wanted so much to go back with them on the bus, but the bus would get back too late.

Harry was tired as he pushed his way through the long,

crowded airport corridors. Kids can do without sleep for days on end, but Harry's groaning body was telling him he couldn't. He checked in at the gate. No assigned seating. He'd have to muscle his way aboard and hope for the best. When the boarding announcement came, Harry moved gingerly and managed a position somewhere in the middle of the line.

He moved on towards the plane and flashed his boarding pass to the shapely stewardess with the ever-ready smile. As he passed through the first class section he caught himself resenting the passengers ensconced in their wide, comfortable seats. He knew that most of them were traveling on expense accounts and that their tax write-off made his tax bite bigger.

The tourist section had that jammed look—seats close together, narrow aisles, cramped leg room. Harry was six feet two and had learned the hard way that an aisle seat on a three-across arrangement was his best bet. The aisle would give his legs a break, and there was always the chance that the middle seat would remain empty for more elbow room and privacy. He spied his seat seven rows back on the right. The window position was occupied by an elderly lady with a hearing aid, already deep in the current issue of *National Geographic*.

Harry collapsed into his seat and loosened his collar. To discourage anyone from getting ideas about that middle seat, he deftly laid his topcoat across it and swung his legs diagonally in front of it.

Secure in his privacy, he touched the overhead light, pulled out his paperback of Frantz Fanon's *The Wretched of the Earth,* and settled in.

The plane kept filling. Friday nights were always tough. Everyone wanted to get home, it seemed.

"Anyone sitting in that seat, brother?" said a massive two-hundred-and-twenty-pounder with an outgoing, friendly face.

Harry shuddered at the prospect. "No," he said limply, "it's not taken." Just his luck to draw a guy like this! If someone had to move in, why couldn't it have been one of those trim, pretty coeds waiting on stand-by?

Harry slipped up and back to let the stranger in. Moments later he dropped into his seat again, angled his legs toward the aisle and found his place in the book. He could feel the press of the newcomer's arm as they elbowed for position on the arm rest. Thank God he was going only to Chicago this flight.

As take-off time approached Harry fumbled for the buckle end of his seat belt, found it, and snapped it firmly into place. When his well-dressed neighbor turned to do the same, Harry's eye caught a small gold cross on the man's lapel. "O God," thought Harry, "a religious type. This might be a long flight after all!"

The jet took off into the wind, circled proudly, headed north and nosed its way to higher altitudes.

When the "Fasten Seat Belt" sign went off, Harry's portly neighbor unsnapped his buckle, put down his copy of *The Wall Street Journal,* and in a cordial manner asked, "Whatcha reading there, brother?"

Harry showed him the cover of his book.

"Hmmm, never heard of it. You read a lot?"

Harry squirmed uncomfortably, like a child being drawn against his will into a Saturday night bath. "Yeah, I like to keep up with things."

"Get to Washington often?" Obviously the man was determined that neither of them would read for awhile.

"No," said Harry, "only been there twice in my life."

"I get there about twice a month. Business. But I tell you this trip took the cake. Darndest thing you ever saw. They had a bunch of agitators blocking traffic, shouting slogans, carrying signs and raising a noisy fuss about Welfare Rights.

"What really ticked me off was the sight of those clergy-men right there in the middle of it all egging the whole thing on! If they'd stick to their own business they wouldn't have time to go around the country stirring things up!"

Harry could feel his stomach muscles tighten. "What *is* their business?" he asked defiantly.

"Brother, that's easy to answer. A minister is supposed to feed people with the bread of life. His job is to visit the sick, teach the young, bury the dead, and help people with their doubts."

"What about *physical* bread?" said Harry. "Doesn't that matter?"

"Sure it matters. But that's politics and economics, not religion. Don't get me wrong, our church does a lot for the poor. We deliver baskets every Thanksgiving and Christmas. We even keep a pantry stocked with canned goods and staples for emergencies. But all this agitation for welfare rights—that's something else. Probably some Communists behind it all."

"Did you ever stop to think what receiving a basket of food does to a human being?" Harry replied. "Don't you think there is a better way to help the casualties of our social and economic system? And don't you think it's the church's busi-ness to help find a better way?"

At this point Harry heard the tinkle of silverware and the sound of tray tables coming into place. Presently, he was looking down at a deliciously attractive meal. He tucked his napkin in between his neck and collar. Bumpy air at meal-time could work havoc with a man's shirt.

As he plunged into his salad, Harry couldn't help noticing that his businessman friend to the right was offering a silent grace, with bowed head, before eating. Harry winced a little at this. He had been raised to return thanks before every meal, but had long since given up doing it in public places. No need to wear your piety on your sleeve! Still, he couldn't help feeling a sense of loss and a twinge of guilt.

The food perked up Harry's spirit. The coffee made him forget his tiredness. As he sank a fork into a cherry cobbler, he turned to his fellow passenger and said, "I think you ought to know that I'm one of those guys that raised your blood pressure. I'm a minister myself. A college chaplain. And I brought a bunch of students to Washington—not because I don't believe in the church, but because I do."

Warming to his cause, Harry went on in an ever-louder voice, "I should think you men in business would want the church to be in there trying to put some flex into the system!"

Harry's tone produced a beep in the old lady's bad ear. She stole a sideward glance, turned down the volume on her hearing aid and went back to her article on a fossil hunt in Nairobi.

"Brother, I like to meet a man who can speak up for his convictions. My name is George Worthington. What's yours?"

Harry told him, and followed with a half-hearted, "Glad to meet you."

"Now about this flex that you talk about," George went on. "Of course, we need justice in the land. The country's in bad shape and lots of people are treated like stepchildren. But listen, Harry, the way to get a just society is by getting men's hearts changed. You get men right with God and watch what happens!"

That argument was suffering from tired blood and Harry could hardly bring himself to listen it out. But George wouldn't be stopped. "If you ordained men would get back to fundamentals and concentrate on leading men to God, and stop cause-hopping all over the place, we might just pull this country together yet."

Harry held out his cup for a refill on coffee and tied into George. "The trouble with guys like you is that you never tell us how many right-with-God types we're going to need before we can have justice. Listen, George, a black man told a bunch of us one day that he'd sooner take his chances in a community of atheists than live in a community of Christians. Why do you suppose he said that? He said that because he had once lived in a town in the Bible Belt where 90 percent of the people went to church and his life was hell.

"Look, George, imagine yourself a minister in a small mining town in West Virginia. For more than a month the miners have been out on strike. Safety standards and wages are the issues. As you watch your people come to church each week, suffering increasingly from the strike, do you mean to tell me that the only thing you'd preach on would be personal religion? Don't you see that life is all one piece? You can't chop it up and make it into airtight compartments like economics, politics, religion. You've got to care about whatever hurts people and drains the life out of them."

George Worthington handed his dinner tray to the stewardess. He was more subdued now, but he wasn't finished. "Harry, if I were that minister in West Virginia, I'd try to keep the morale of my people high. I'd talk about courage and perseverance. I'd remind them that some day soon they'd enter into a life on the other side of death where the true believer wouldn't want for anything."

"Just as I thought," said Harry. "You'd try to get them to be strong and good *within* the system—but you wouldn't say a word or do a thing to *improve* the system."

"Harry, Harry, the system has always been corrupt. Don't be so naïve. You can't make it perfect."

"I agree," said Harry. "The system is not perfectable. But it is improvable. The fundamental difference between us is that you think Christ came to deliver us from the world. I say he came to free us from our sins and hang-ups in order that we might work with him for the redemption of the world. My focus is *this* life. Yours is the life to *come*—as far as your religion goes."

"Harry, if we started moving on the hot issues of the day in my church we'd split the congregation. There's enough conflict in business and government and on television. Who needs it in the church?"

"So you take the easy way out. You meet as a church around bland and harmless causes. The world's pain never penetrates your reveries. What a price for internal peace! It's churches like yours that make my job tough. Kids know a copout when they see one."

The passenger in front of Harry decided to catch up on his sleep. His seat came back into Harry's lap and made him feel as if he were pinned in a phone booth.

George's voice was quiet as he spoke. The bluster was gone. "Harry, damn it all, I know underneath you're right. My two sons are away at the university now and neither of them goes near the chapel. Both raised in the church, too."

George slipped a well-manicured hand inside his suit coat and pulled out a color photo of his family. Harry admired it and passed it back.

"Harry, let me tell you something that I seldom talk about to anyone. I'm a lonely man, desperately lonely. That lovely woman in the picture, the dream girl of my life, died a year ago this month. Cancer. With her gone and the boys away, life just hasn't been the same for me.

"Do you know what keeps me going? My trust in God. I don't miss a day reading the Bible and kneeling down to pray. Jesus is more real to me today than he was the day I was confirmed.

"The kind of faith that you're too busy and involved to

share is all I have. Don't forget, Harry, no matter how big society is, we experience life's crisis points alone. No one can be born in my place, or believe in my place, or die in my place."

George's eyes were moist as he said, "If I had never met Jesus, I don't know where I'd be."

Presently, the "Fasten Seat Belt" sign came on. Harry got back all the room he'd paid for when the passenger in front brought his seat straight up. The drone of the landing gear dropping into place signaled that the plane would soon be touching down.

Harry turned to George, put out a hand, and said, "I'm sorry that you lost your wife and mighty glad for your sake that somewhere along the way you came to faith in Christ.

"There are two wings on this plane, George, and both are needed to put this baby up. And there are two sides to biblical religion, too. It isn't all public action. It isn't all personal comfort and assurance. It's both. Agreed?"

"Agreed."

The little lady put her magazine away and turned the knob on her hearing aid. She smiled toward her neighbor in the middle and chided him gently. "George, you never gave us your boys' names or told us what school they're in!"

CHAPTER 13

What Makes Christian
Social Action Different?

Turbulent periods of history have a disturbing way of putting men and institutions on the spot. They demand involvement and decision. They smoke us out of our sanctuaries, compel us to take sides, disengage us from routine, and deny us the luxury of a long look. Will you or won't you? Yes or no? Where do you stand? These are the questions that press for answers when the tide rolls in and angry waters lap at the walls of our castles in the sand. We live in such a period now. And for the church it is an anxious and trying time, and yet, a time of promise.

Believing that Jesus Christ is the Lord of history, churches and churchmen have plunged into a variety of political and social issues. In some cases they have maintained a distinct Christian identity. In most instances they have joined with others of like mind in quest of a common goal. And this is as it should be. D. L. Munby is quoted with approval by Lesslie Newbigin when he says, "The secular world has its limited aims, and God respects these. There are no other alternative aims for Christians in their everyday life. But Christians, believing in God, can see these aims as *limited*, precisely because they look for *ultimate* satisfaction to God Alone." [1]

But whether we work apart or in connection with others to make our witness in the field of social action, it is important to ask, What makes Christian social action different? Is there a plus that we bring to such activity? "What do ye more than others?" was Jesus' question to his disciples. It may be his question to us today.

Ideally, Christians ought to bring to social action a unique perspective. Our concerns should never be restricted to the few issues of the day that have captured the public imagination. The modern missionary movement, so much maligned by contemporary crusaders, at least had the merit of expressing the compassion of Jesus Christ on a wide variety of fronts and in a variety of ways: education, agriculture, medicine, literacy, publications, co-ops, orphanages, refugee care, clothing, to mention some. The one-cause man in our society, with all due respect for his ardor, must not be allowed to intimidate us or decatholicize our passion.

One of the things I enjoy doing when I have a bit of time in our city of New York is to drop in on a radio store downtown. I find the window displays almost irresistible: short wave, standard broadcast, AM, FM—they are all there. Occasionally you will see someone come in to purchase, let's say, a portable radio. He asks the clerk if he might try it. The man gives it to him. He flips it on and the station comes in with great force. This radio sells for $9.94. A few minutes later he picks one up that sells for $49.94, turns it on and finds that the station is rather weak and crackly. He is tempted to conclude that the first radio is the better of the two. What he doesn't know is that the first radio is bringing in a station whose transmitter is just ten blocks away, while the other one is bringing in a station from Hartford, Connecticut! I am suggesting that across the years, making all due allowances for ghastly missionary miscalculations, the Christian church has sought to pick up signals on a wider band of need than the one-cause specialist.

The one-cause man can always embarrass us. He can come from a denominational board of religious education to speak to the assembled teachers of a given church, ask "What have you done lately for the cradle roll?" and make his listeners cringe. Carrying only this portfolio, he can shame an entire faculty with his knowledge and concern. A freshman who had just discovered civil rights at Ann Arbor came bursting into my study to ask whether I would be at his rally that night at ten. I told him I couldn't be. Immediately he expressed grave doubt about my passion. To restore some balance in the conversation I asked him what he had done for the orphans in Hong Kong lately. Why not? God's love goes out in equal measure to all men, and God wills that all men, wherever they might be, should be delivered from whatever it is that holds them down.

This, then, is to express concern about the zealots in our midst, whether in society at large or in the church, who set up arbitrary tests of relevance. This is the issue and this is the way to do it, they state, without allowing the possibility that others might feel strongly about another issue or another way of doing the same thing. Jesus had a methodological fundamentalist in his group by the name of John, who came running to him, saying, " 'Teacher, we saw a man casting out demons in your name, and we forbade him, because he was not following us.' But Jesus said, 'Do not forbid him; for no one who does a mighty work in my name will be able soon after to speak evil of me. For he that is not against us is for us' " (Mark 9:38–40, RSV).

I remind you that Jacques Ellul insists that most of our social passion is quite subjective and highly selective. Christians are forever jumping on the bandwagon of that which is popular. Ellul argues that we ought to be going after injustices that few others are sensitive to. He goes so far as to suggest that when a cause gets popular it's time for us to leave it in the hands of others and move on.

In one of the first women's suffrage parades in New York it is said that 89 brave men dared to march. After women's suffrage had been adopted, another parade was held in celebration. The original small group of men was invited to march in one section. On the day of the festivities all 520 of the original 89 appeared!

Let's not take ourselves so seriously as to feel that we have the only leads on what needs to be done or the primary knowledge as to how the goal should best be attained. Within the kingdom of God there is a variety of dispositions and sensitivities.

Let me move on to suggest that Christian social action is unique in that its ultimate aim is reconciliation. Surely it must be acknowledged that precious few reforms ever effected in our world were won without conflict of one sort or another—confrontations, showdowns, divisions, polarizations. Though the Christian man may have to go this route, as I believe he does at present on many contemporary issues, always for him this will be an interim tactic. For he believes in the marrow of his being that God wills to reconcile all things to himself in heaven and on earth in Jesus Christ. However impassioned he may be as he signs petitions or writes

his senator or marches on Washington, he will have room
in his heart and prayers for both sides of the struggle: for
the slumlord as well as the tenant, for the hawk as well as
the dove, for the corporation executive as well as the worker,
for the university trustee as well as the student, for the pusher
as well as the addict.

Finally, the Christian ought to be able to bring to social
action the quality of perseverance. Social passion has a short
life-expectancy. It claims us in our youth in a big way, then
gently fades away. (And how it claims us, especially in our
university years!) The university freshman from a Republican
home will usually have become a Democrat by the time
Thanksgiving comes.

One is not selling short the considerable vision and grasp
of reality that is present on the various campuses of our
country on such issues as war and peace, poverty and wealth,
and new priorities. It is a sobering thought, however, to ask
one's self where these students will be ten years hence.
Chances are that by 1984 they will have been absorbed into
the system and grown comfortable with its benefits. There
aren't many old liberals in the world. Bertrand Russell was
a glittering exception. Every so often we stumble upon one who
is independently wealthy, or one who has manned his post
for years behind the barricades of academic tenure. But for
most, the passion seems to spend itself before the job is done.
Leopold Tyrmand, writing in *The New Yorker,* said, "Though
nothing keeps us from pursuing what we consider right and
fighting against what we see as wrong, the task does become
boring after thirty-five." [2]

The pressures are hard to live with. Josiah Holland once
observed that "every man who strikes blows for power, for
influence, for institutions, for the right, must be just as good
an anvil as he is a hammer." At times the seeming futility

of what we do causes us to pull back. I was struck the other day by Leonard Woolf's view of his life's work. "I see clearly," he said, "that I have achieved practically nothing. The world today and the history of the human anthill during the past 57 years would be exactly the same as it is if I had played ping pong instead of sitting on committees and writing books and memoranda. I have therefore to make the rather ignominious confession that I must have in a long life ground through between 150,000 and 200,000 hours of perfectly useless work." [3]

Christians can overcome the tendency to drop back. Their motivation is dual, not single. Yes, like the humanist, they are motivated by the cry of the man who says, "*Come* and help." But, unlike the humanist, they are also motivated by the voice of Jesus, saying, "*Go* and help." The happy thing about Christian social action is that it is theologically funded and thus has the prospect of greater durability.

The word *eschatology* is bandied about these days but seldom defined. Listen to this definition of eschatology by a brilliant Old Testament man, T. C. Vriezen: "Eschatology is the expression of the belief that God holds history in the hollow of His hand, and that He will make the history of the world end in complete communion between God and man, so that He will come as King; or, in other words, so that He may be all in all." [4] It is in this confidence that we *mount* up with wings as eagles; that we are able to *run* and not weary; that we are empowered to *walk* . . . and *walk* . . . and *walk,* and not faint!

A church member should never say to a minister who is going off to serve as counselor at a youth camp for a week, "Have a good time and enjoy yourself." For there is no such camp that I have ever heard of where anything like six hours of sleep, not to mention eight, is allowed the faculty. Some-

how the young have a way of rising at five for the morning
dip, going at top speed all day, and talking or pillow fighting
into the wee hours of the morning. During one such experience years ago we sought to quiet the campers down a bit at
bedtime and inject a devotional note by having them get
ready for bed and then come out around a grassy rectangle
for a brief period of group singing. We would sing a popular
song or two, and then a hymn, and then conclude with
Malotte's setting of the Lord's Prayer. I can still remember
across the twenty intervening years the lift I felt within my
soul when those young voices, unafraid of the highest notes
and unaccompanied, moved on to the climactic measures,
"For Thine is the kingdom, and the power, and the glory,
forever."

Because this is so, we of all people can live with deferred
results if need be, for we know that the end will come, that
the end is good, that it belongs to God. This is what Auden
was suggesting in his "Christmas Oratorio" when he wrote,

Let us therefore be contrite but without anxiety,
For Powers and Times are not Gods but mortal gifts from God;
Let us acknowledge our defeats but without despair,
For all societies and epochs are transient details,
Transmitting an everlasting opportunity
That the Kingdom of Heaven may come, not in our present
And not in our future, but in the Fullness of Time.
Let us pray.[5]

Closing Prayer

God, as we strive to do the right
     in the public sector,
Give us direction, enthusiasm,
     and good sense.

Save us from arrogance
and hasty judgment.
Help us to unite passion
and reason.

And more than all—grant that in
what we champion and how we
go about it
We may glorify Thy name.
Through Jesus Christ our Lord.
Amen.

CHAPTER 14

Divine Judgment and
American Unrest

"Shall I not punish them for these things?
              says the Lord,
and shall I not avenge myself
on a nation such as this?"

Jeremiah 5:29, RSV

Sometimes a minister preaches because it's Sunday. More often, one would hope, he preaches because he has something to say and will have no rest until he says it. What I must share today is a conviction that stalked me for months and finally cornered me. Because at this stage it is hardly more than an insistent intuition, it may suffer as it translates from feeling into speech. The conviction, simply stated, is this: America is a nation under divine judgment.

That we suffer unrest as a people hardly needs elaboration. People with axes to grind are everywhere. Belligerence is the prevailing mood. Mistrust and suspicion are rampant. A depressing variety of gaps separate us one from the other. We have a way of talking past each other rather than to or with each other. And with sickening frequency we resort to violence either to guard what we have or to get what we want.

Unrest? If anything, this term is too mild to describe the American experience.

The accepted explanations are helpful as far as they go, but they don't reach far enough. You know them by now, these stock explanations: The population has exploded and we haven't learned yet how to cope with what this means. Technological advances have whisked us out of the familiar into the new and caught us unprepared. Communism has played upon the prejudices of the Third World and stirred it up against us. The institutions that were meant to serve us have become fossilized and insensitive.

But there is a further explanation for what is happening to us. This further explanation does not displace the others, but it may be more to the point than they. Simply put, we are suffering for our sins. The accepted explanations that are so very much in vogue today have one thing in common: they leave out the moral factor and overlook man's sin. They score the need to update education, to accept change, to eliminate or contain communism, to humanize our institutions; but they fail to suggest that the picture can be viewed within the framework of command and disobedience, judgment and grace.

It is one thing for outright humanists and gung-ho rationalists to reject this framework. But how can Christians reject it without abandoning the biblical perspective? It's not that the horizontal factors should be ignored. They are there and they are real. But they are not the only forces at work in history. Man can sin! God can judge! And judgment can happen within history as well as at the end of history.

Some of our religious leaders are so taken by contemporary human culture that they forget the tension that prevails between God and the world. One gets the impression that ever since God read Spock he's gone permissive. Avarice, lust, hatred, vengeance, indifference mean nothing to him. If we could speak of evil, not sin, and trace our anguish to such abstractions as structures and the times rather than the human heart, we could dispense with the concept of judgment.

But this would not free us from the effects of judgment. Looking back over twenty years in the ministry, I see that I have tried to teach myself and my people how to recognize and respond to mercy. But I have never taught myself or my people how to recognize or respond to judgment. What does it look like when it comes? How do we know when we are in it?

Judgment is visited in many ways. In the days of Noah, judgment meant physical destruction. In eighth century B.C. Israel, judgment meant deportation and assimilation. In Rome, judgment meant being taken over by barbaric hordes from the north.

But the model that best fits our situation is the Tower of Babel saga. The people in that story were determined to build a tower that would touch the sky in order that they might have a city and a name. It is very instructive that in the Genesis account there were no outside hordes, there was no physical destruction, no one was carted off. What did happen was that the people simply could not bring off what they wanted to bring off. They were confounded. Their purposes were frustrated. And they became tragically divided. Given our sin, we would be this way if there were no population explosion; if there were no technological revolution; if there were no communism; and if there were no sclerotic bureaucracy.

We are a nation under divine judgment. Our unrest testifies to the inherent instability of a God-flouting, man-centered society. Jeremiah had a sensitive heart and a deep love for his people, yet he could not answer the Almighty when God said, "Shall I not punish them for these things? And shall I not avenge myself on a nation such as this?" America is not Israel, I know. But the church in America purports to be on the same continuum with the Old Testament community. It is possible for a people, despite their lofty self-image, to exhaust the divine patience and be shut up to the consequences of their sin.

It may be that our greed has finally caught up with us. I fear it true that "the only ideal the West cherishes is economic growth." [1] Why else would we encourage people to go to college on the basis of a $100,000 lifetime differential over the man who does not go? Why else would a radio chain instruct its newscasters not to elaborate on the possibility of stormy weather because such elaborations are bad for business? In our society we judge a man by what he has and not by what he is. This norm bears testimony to the greed under which we live.

Perhaps our tolerance for perversion and promiscuity has finally caught up with us. I have been accused of many things in the ministry, but no one has ever accused me of being a prude. However, when I walk around New York City—especially in the Times Square area—I find myself wondering how long this nation will exist with such rottenness at its heart. There have always been movie houses in that area trafficking in the lewd and sensual. But matters now are worse. These houses have set up miniature screens outside so that the more salacious episodes of what is going on inside can be seen by everyone who passes, regardless of age.

Don't tell me that there are critics who call this art. Every degenerating society has doubtless been able to come up with critics ready to define a vice as a virtue in the name of art. I am sure that in Sodom and Gomorrah before the end came there were men of stature, well-lettered and well-credentialed, who mistook licentiousness for progress. If there are human beings who must see lurid films let them form private clubs and view to their hearts' content. But shame on a city where a man and wife cannot walk with their children without having to fend off such filth.

And it may be that our violence has caught up with us. We've become hardened to violence, haven't we? Our arousal point keeps getting higher and higher. And even when finally aroused we cannot sustain our indignation very long. I heard a chap say the other day that ours is a three-day society. He meant that when something ghastly tragic happens it is headlined the first day; reduced to the back section the second day; and confined to a squib the third day. By the fourth day, we've washed it out of our minds.

As a case in point, most of us have already dismissed the My Lai massacre. The self-justification of the military has prevailed. We can be reminded that 40,000 Americans have died in the longest war in this nation's history and go out and shop for bargains five minutes later. We can be told that 25,000 Americans die each year because of drunks behind the wheels of automobiles and then go on with what we're doing. And what shall we say of that community in the Northwest, recently in the news, whose major industry is the making and storing of lethal gases for the Defense Department? Citizens of that town were queried on how they were enjoying life. Most, it turned out, are quite happy. Apparently if a man's pipe is drawing well, and his grass is clipped, and he has eliminated all the ghosts on his television screen, and is keeping up with the payments on his home—all is well!

We keep playing word games with violence. When the other side does it, it's violence; but when our side does it, it's a legitimate expression of force. And all of it is a farce. In a sense, in today's football game the Minnesota Vikings and the Kansas City Chiefs will be on opposite sides. But in deeper fact, they are both on the same side in that both are believers in and practitioners of professional football. Likewise, from outward appearances it would look as though the Weatherman faction of the SDS and the Chicago police force are on opposite sides. In actual fact, they are on the same side in that both are believers in and practitioners of violence. And it may be—I do not know—that God feels we've been playing this game long enough.

That is why we cannot overcelebrate the insights and passion of Martin Luther King, Jr. At a time when it would have been the simplest thing óf all for him to capitulate to violence and feed upon the legitimate grievances of his people, he sought the path of nonviolence. From the other side of the Atlantic the Frenchman Jacques Ellul commented thus on King's position: "To be on the side of the oppressed and at the same time have to tell them that their explosions of violence are futile and will bring no real change—this is the most thankless position anyone can take. It was the position of Martin Luther King, and we know how vulnerable it is. It was also the position of Jesus in relation to the Pharisees (who wanted to organize resistance to the Romans) and the Zealots." [2] Dr. King chose to move in the succession of John the beloved, Saint Francis, Ghandi, and Schweitzer—and we killed him!

What do we do if we are under judgment? We can recognize that such is the case, that it is one of the fundamental facts of our existence, and stop trying to define our situation apart from it. And maybe if we kept in mind that we are all in this pressure cooker together, we would be a little easier on each other—instead of going around short-fused and irritable.

And we can make it a point to resist all propaganda that is designed to justify either ourselves or our nation— even when it is wrapped in the flag.

But, thank God, we can also repent. It's not just judgment we are under, it's *divine* judgment! And this is our hope, for God's judgment is not vindictive, but restorative and curative. It moves always in the direction of reconciliation. Jeremiah had no answer to the questions, "Shall I not punish them for these things? And shall I not avenge myself on a nation such as this?" He could, however, come back and say out of a broken heart, "Yet thou, O Lord, art in the midst of us, and we are called by thy name; leave us not" (Jer. 14:9b, RSV). Just as our unrest stems in large measure from divine judgment, so our rest is to be found in divine grace.

Patrick Kirby put it this way:

> Only out of chaos
> Creation;
> Only out of confusion
> Order
> Only from our decay,
> The new shoots of a New Earth;
> Only out of our darkness
> Light unquenchable,
> And a new Heaven
> Filled with new stars! [3]

Closing Prayer

> Revive the world, O God,
>   beginning with America.
> Revive America
>   beginning with the church.
> Revive the church, O God,
>   beginning with me.
>   Through Jesus Christ our Lord.
>   **Amen.**

CHAPTER 15

Christmas—Live and in Color

Whoever does not receive the kingdom of God like a child shall not enter it.

Mark 10:15

Not long ago the Columbia Broadcasting System announced a startling breakthrough. It is now possible to make color movies from black and white film. The work on this project was done in the CBS Laboratories in nearby Stamford, Connecticut. What is sorely needed now is a process by which human experience can be transformed from a dull black and white into living color. This is especially true of our experience of Christmas, that will be long on motion and short on meaning, a celebration that will be more extensive than intensive.

How easily one can be engrossed in the protocol of the season. After all, there are cards to be sent and received. There is a gift list to balance. There are parties to arrange. There are homecomings and homegoings to anticipate. But to settle for this kind of Christmas only is like settling for black and white when we might have living color.

127

I argue that, given the state of the world these days, not to mention the malnutrition of the inner man, we cannot afford such a Christmas. "I want a real Advent this year," said the woman in the hospital to her pastor. She meant, "I want to get with this hope business." Some pious fraud had rebuked her weeping saying, "Have you no faith?" "Faith?" she screamed it back. "I have third generation faith. But it has not saved me from this despair. I want an Advent." [1]

Shortly after color television came into West Germany, officials in Saarbrücken received an angry note from a husband and wife who complained that they were still receiving their pictures in black and white. The officials tactfully replied that the couple had to have a color set to receive pictures in color. The trouble was not in the transmission; it was in the reception.

The word that just might bring us over from dullness to awareness is that intriguing, well-known word of Jesus, a word found in each of the Synoptic Gospels: "Whoever does not receive the kingdom of God like a child shall not enter therein" (Mark 10:15). Jesus was drawn to children and children were drawn to Jesus. He referred to the way they played funeral and wedding in the market place. He refused to silence them that day in the temple when they were crying "Hosanna," choosing instead to rebuke the chief priests and scribes, "Have you never read, 'Out of the mouths of babes and sucklings thou hast brought perfect praise'?" (Matt. 21:16b, RSV). On one occasion he set a child in the midst of the temple, thereby suggesting that one of the standards by which institutionalized religion is to be measured is its effect on a child.

"Whoever does not receive the kingdom of God like a child shall not enter therein." Jesus, of course, was not putting a premium on childishness. There is a difference between childishness and childlikeness. We must leave childishness behind. In St. Paul's poem to love, 1 Corinthians 13, he acknowledges that whereas he once spoke like a child, thought like a child, understood like a child, as a man he had put away childish things. He goes on in the next chapter of that same letter to plead that his hearers "in understanding be men." Gerhard Ebeling puts it that "the faith that is afraid to think is unbelief in the mask of piety." [2]

"Whosoever does not receive the kingdom of God like a child shall not enter therein." If I understand our Lord correctly, he is suggesting that there is a marked correlation between the spirit of a child and the spirit of authentic religious experience.

Why did Jesus make such an analogy? Perhaps because children are not very often stymied by self-consciousness. They have no image to project—unless they've been tampered with by one of us. They have a way of responding and reacting to life freely. They show elation or disappointment readily. Their lives are marked by spontaneity and unpredictability. They wear their hearts on their sleeves. They are not coy or devious. They are transparent, almost totally uninhibited.

It is something of this that Jesus wishes us to feel and experience as we reach out after God. Our life experiences are thin when they might be thick if only we were not so frequently saddled with self-consciousness. We seem obsessed by the notion that we must respond to life in a manner that is consistent with our image. We would much rather be considered proper and right than run the risk of open and inductive living. Presently, this desire to be consistent with one's image leads to falsifying our reactions to life. We are not at liberty to respond according to the feeling we know in the innermost ring of our being. Albert Lasker, who has been described as the father of modern advertising and a man who really should have known, said, "Remember that a truly honest man creates a variety of impressions. When everybody gets the same reaction to a fellow I distrust him immediately. He's playing a part. He's creating that impression deliberately!" [3]

I'm suggesting that one of the things that keeps us living on the prosaic level of black and white instead of on the brilliant level of live color is the fear of breaking with an adopted or assigned image. "I'm a college graduate—college graduates don't get excited about God." "I'm a businessman —businessmen aren't supposed to depend openly on prayer." "I'm a scientist—scientists don't take miracle seriously." "I'm a teenager—teenagers are supposed to be bored by church." "I'm a military man—military men aren't supposed to question war." At the birth of Jesus Christ reactions were unrestrained. Angels sang! Shepherds ran! Wise men saddled up and rode! Herod raged! Sympathies were loosed and expressed!

"Whosoever does not receive the kingdom of God like a little child shall not enter therein." Perhaps Jesus urged this analogy upon us because children have a way of living each experience as it comes. They are not concerned to relate *this* experience to the *last* one or the *next* one. They are not driven by a need to be consistent. They live the now moment intimately, deeply. They have an enviable way of knowing how to savor the present. Dr. S. I. Hayakawa, the beleaguered acting president of San Francisco State College in 1968, knew calmer days years ago in the city of Chicago. One day he took his children to visit family friends in a large apartment house that was serviced by automatic elevators. His main concern was to board the elevator, get upstairs, and begin to talk with these friends. The children, however, began to savor the "now" moment that the self-service elevator afforded. They were enthralled by the lights, the buttons, the feeling of motion and power. Hayakawa acknowledged that what was only a means to him was a live and intensely interesting moment for his children. Maybe this is something of what Jesus had in mind.

The enemies here are many. One is familiarity. "I don't get excited; I've been here before." This is a grave temptation for ministers, especially those of us who are professional handlers of the Holy. We've been there before. That was good advice that the veteran missionary gave to the young couple going out. "Take whatever pictures you're going to take in the first six months, for after that you'll forget what the folks back home would like to see." You'll become accustomed to the flora and fauna of that new place and lose your ability to wonder and marvel at it all. Eric Hoffer claims that he has always tried to live life as though he were a tourist. Perhaps this is why there is something exciting in most everything that Hoffer says or writes.

I'm convinced that the writer of Ecclesiastes must have been suffering from a peptic ulcer when he said, "All is vanity. . . . There is nothing new under the sun" (Eccles. 1:2, 9, RSV). I doubt that he had ever really been present at life. You know how it goes; when you've seen one museum you've seen them all. When you've been to Christmas once, you've been there for all times. Familiarity.

Another enemy, more subtle, is the tendency of literate people to systematize and analyze their experiences. It belongs to our maturity that we step back from life to locate and define ourselves, to reflect on where we've been and where we are. But there comes a point in the life of the intellectualized Christian when he becomes more intent on classifying an experience than having it. He wants to get it down on paper in black and white. He gets to the place where he plays theological scrabble with something that ought to be lived.

Anton Boisen has written: "The secondhandedness of the learned world is the secret of its mediocrity. . . . Every intellectual revolution which has ever stirred humanity into greatness has been a passionate protest against inert ideas. . . . Our goal is to see the immediate events of our lives as instances of our general ideas." Children have the experience first and the explanation later—if ever. We reverse the order, which is one reason we shy away from miracle.

What is miracle but "event ahead of explanation"? When men, instead of being vividly present at any occasion, become once removed in the role of pious analysts, we have the making of that saddest of all sights, the theologian who no longer says his prayers. Socrates is credited with observing that "the unexamined life is not worth living." There's another way of looking at the matter: "The unlived life is not worth examining." When Moses saw the bush aflame, he turned aside to see. When shepherds got word of the nativity of Christ they said, "Let us go over to Bethlehem and see this thing that has happened, which the Lord has made known to us" (Luke 2:15, RSV).

"Whosoever does not receive the kingdom of God like a child shall not enter therein." Perhaps Jesus was urging this analogy upon us because children are so consistently free of worldly care. They go too far, to be sure, for if we were all as careless as they, we would be in trouble. They care too little, perhaps, but we care far too much. We are entirely too preoccupied with our cash value, wondering whether our breath and our money will expire at the same time. Children trust their mothers and fathers for their needs. Even in the dark days of the depression we trusted. Jesus is saying, in effect, I want you to trust God the way those children trust you. He said it plainly. "Take no thought, saying, What shall we eat?

or, What shall we drink? or, Wherewithal shall we be clothed? (For after all these things do the Gentiles seek:) for your heavenly Father knoweth that ye have need of all these things. But seek ye first the kingdom of God, and his righteousness; and all these things shall be added unto you" (Matt. 6:31–33, KJV). It is the burden of worldly care that keeps us shut out to the glory, color and wonder of God.

I was proud of the man who joined me in a flight from Detroit to Minneapolis one night. It was obvious that he had had a few to stiffen his courage. He was reaching for strength to play the hand that life had dealt him. A CPA with a salary of thirty thousand a year, he had just gone to a new firm and wasn't sure that he had the credentials that would enable him to be successful. The arrangements had just been made. He won me to his side when he said, "I'm going home but I don't want my family to know that I have any concern about this at all." He went on to describe his wife, his children, his church. He was practicing what I would call the "bulkhead" theory of worry. Bulkheads are built into ships in order to keep a leak in one portion of the hull from filling the whole vessel with water. Granted, there are worries that belong to our worldly existence, but in the name of God, let us seal them off and contain them lest a concern for security and income should mar our reception of all that God is trying to say and do. It is precisely this that Browning had in mind when he said:

> Because a man has shop to mind
> In time and place, since flesh must live,
> Needs spirit lack all life behind,
> All stray thoughts, fancies fugitive,
> All loves except what trade can give?
>
> I want to know a butcher paints,
> A baker rhymes for his pursuit,

Candlestick-maker much acquaints
His soul with song, or, haply mute,
Blows out his brains upon the flute!

But—shop each day and all day long!
Friend, your good angel slept, your star
Suffered eclipse, fate did you wrong!
From where these sorts of treasures are,
There should our hearts be—Christ, how far! [4]

"Whosoever does not receive the kingdom of God like a child shall not enter therein." What we need is a second childhood, a rebirth of wonder. We need to open out on the word made flesh. Perhaps on this storm-ridden day we should go home and read the Nativity stories in a new translation, or lie on the floor and listen to the sweep of Handel's *Messiah,* or open ourselves to the Nativity in art or drama until the color and dynamic of God's coming gets through.

D. H. Lawrence can experience more in an apple than most of us can experience in the grace of God. He writes: "They call all experience of the senses mystic, when the experience is considered. So an apple becomes mystic when I taste in it the summer and the snows, the wild welter of earth and the insistence of the sun. All of which things I can surely taste in a good apple." [5] Here we are with the wonder of God's love made flesh.

"The theological student fresh out of theological school asked the little man, 'And what is your ultimate concern?' The little man, having also read Tillich, replied with a sigh, 'That the Ultimate be concerned about me.' " [6]

The Ultimate is, and this is the wonder and glory of it all. I wish for you as I wish for myself, a Christmas live and in color. Auden in his work "For the Time Being" has the shepherds gathered around the manger say:

Tonight for the first time the prison gates
Have opened.
Music and sudden light
Have interrupted our routine tonight,
And swept the filth of habit from our hearts.
O here and now our endless journey starts.[7]

Closing Prayer

Lord, we know the words,
    Teach us now the music of our faith.
We know the forms of celebration
    Give us now the fire,
    the passion and the joy.

Break through the curtain of our dark
    And help us to receive Thee unashamed
    with the abandon of a little child.
In our Savior's name we pray.
                                    Amen.

CHAPTER 16

The Outside and the Inn

. . . because there was no place for them in the inn.

Luke 2:7b, RSV

It wasn't the Bethlehem Hilton, to be sure, but whatever its name and size, the inn that failed to accommodate Joseph and Mary two thousand years ago is familiar to more people than the most widely advertised hotel in the world. We all have a personalized mental picture of that inn, and a particular set of feelings that asserts itself when we come to that line in the Nativity story, "And she gave birth to her first-born son . . . and laid him in a manger, because there was no place for them in the inn" (Luke 2:7, RSV).

Should ever the site of that inn be identified with certainty by archaeologists, preachers around the world should be taxed for its restoration because of all the sermons it has given them. Most of these sermons, I fear, have been neither fair nor realistic. My writing may be no better.

The usual characterization makes the innkeeper a villain in the piece and the registered guests unwitting accomplices.

But let me take the innkeeper's part for a moment. Because of Mary's condition it is likely that she and Joseph arrived late. What was the innkeeper to do, evict a paid-up guest to accommodate two new strangers? Perhaps in the dark he could not discern that Mary was with child. Perhaps he never saw or spoke to either of them. Some employee out front, or a posted sign, could have made it quite clear that no more room was available.

As for the guests, it was probably the case that not one of them knew what was going on. Guests as a rule do not determine hotel policy or participate in its application. To make that anonymous businessman the prototype of Christ-rejection is at once unwarranted and unjust.

"She gave birth to her first-born son and laid him in a manger, because there was no place for them in the inn." We are on firmer ground when we approach the subject by asking what Jesus' being born in a stable tells us about God and his ways with men. We may assume that if ever providence operated anywhere, it operated in the arrangements that surrounded Jesus' birth. Details of time and place and manner were not left to chance. Why then the stable and not the inn?

Because God has a way of coming into history from the outside—from outside our theological systems, our social and religious institutions, our ingrown patterns and ways of doing. Let the inn, therefore, represent the Establishment, and let us learn from that first Christmas that God, more likely than not, will come to us without benefit of Establishment succor or support. Paul understood this. In his first letter to the Christians at Corinth he noted that, "to shame the wise, God . . . has chosen things low and contemptible, mere nothings, to overthrow the existing order" (1 Cor. 1:27, 28, NEB).

And this, not because God is capricious, but because man

from the beginning has sought to capture, control, and exploit the holy; to identify God with his own interests, to make God party to his purposes, to blunt God's truth by intimacy and familiarity—in short, to take God over.

God never leaves himself without a witness. But when you stop to think about it, you realize that from the very beginning the witnesses have a way of coming not from the *inn* but from the *outside*.

James Sanders has reminded us recently that the first lesson in morality recorded anywhere in the Bible came from an outsider. Abraham had passed his wife Sarah off in Egypt as his sister. He was reprimanded in these words by Pharaoh: "What is this that you have done to me? . . . Why did you say, 'She is my sister,' so that I took her for my wife?" (Gen. 12:18,19, RSV). This is a voice from outside faith correcting the father of the faithful.

It was the outside voice of Elijah that nettled Ahab and Jezebel as they were established in their royalty. It was the people of Nineveh who responded to Jonah's appeal for repentance. It was Ruth from the pagan land of Moab who gave to the Jews returned from exile their most convincing demonstration of love.

And in the New Testament the pattern continues. The forerunner of Jesus was not a conventional Pharisee or Sadducee, but a voice crying in the wilderness. It was a Roman centurion who prompted Jesus to say, "Not even in Israel have I found such faith" (Luke 7:9b, RSV). They were Greeks who came to Andrew during Holy Week and said, "Sir, we would see Jesus" (John 12:21, KJV). It was a Samaritan rather than a priest or Levite who saved the helpless man that day. And in the early church it was an outsider, Saul of Tarsus, who caught the vision of divine grace and set the Christian cause in motion.

We keep looking to the inn for our salvation, but the Savior waits outside. Large corporations often go outside for their chief executives lest by promoting from within they become perilously inbred. The salvation of public education in this city is more likely than not to come from voices outside the inn of the Establishment. Institutions that really want their efficiency evaluated call in an outside firm.

I participated a while ago in a panel on preaching with three other ministers. The subject was the future of preaching. It was the dullest panel that you could imagine. If preaching has someplace to go, as perhaps it does, it will only learn where it should go and what it should be about by listening to the outside. The answer will not come from within the preaching establishment. When George E. Reedy was press secretary to President Johnson, he was appalled by the fact that the president, no matter what his party, was spared direct contact with critical voices from without. He has given us his findings in a book ominously titled *The Twilight of the Presidency*. It was a youthful outside voice in the well-known fairy tale that told the king that he was naked.

Perhaps by now you are able to sense why I am troubled about our Christmases. It would almost appear that we had Jesus in captivity, that we were holding him by virtue of our hospitality toward him. We assume that Christ is in the inn with us. That is a fatal assumption.

Our celebrations of Christmas are usually aesthetically pleasing and neatly engineered. We have a way of postponing the questions that the Christ child came to raise. Our various rites and services are designed to minimize the differences between God's holy will and our imperfect ways.

I suppose it is all right now to quote from *The Catcher in the Rye*. Do you remember that passage where Holden takes his girlfriend to see the colorful Christmas extravaganza at

Radio City? The lights are there, the sound of well-tuned instruments, the hidden wires, the motion, the activity, the song, dramatic curtain effects, and first-rate professional staging. But Holden sees through it. "Old Jesus probably would've puked if He could see it," he says, "—all those fancy costumes and all. The thing Jesus really would've liked would be the guy that plays the kettledrum in the orchestra." [1]

The homelessness of Jesus is the source of his power over men! "He hath no place to lay his head" (Matt. 8:20b). Not in your ideology or mine. Not in your theology or mine. Not in your church or mine. "He hath no place to lay his head." He is not in the inn of black theology or white supremacy, either one. He is not in the inn of laissez-faire capitalism or the socialist state. He is not in the inn of the American dream or Soviet Russia's latest ten-year plan. To all of these he is outside. And this is our salvation and our hope.

God did not come in Jesus Christ to ratify our judgments, to confirm our values, to help us fulfill our wishes. Rather, he came as one outside to bring the light of God to bear on all our strivings.

"She gave birth to her first-born son . . . and laid him in a manger, because there was no place for them in the inn" (Luke 2:7a, RSV). That's where he is, outside. And that's where we must go to find him, outside.

I had the pleasure of studying some years ago at Princeton Seminary under a man now deceased who was an eminent authority in homiletics, Andrew W. Blackwood. His son, Andrew, Jr., a distinguished preacher in his own right, has given us a poem about Christmas which expresses poignantly the burden of this chapter:

> Jesus, what have you done to us?
>   we wanted a pet kitten

and you turned into a tiger
　　we liked you the way you were
why couldn't you leave us alone?

We wanted you to show up when we wanted
　　you to make us feel good
We wanted a pretty church for weddings and
　　baptisms and funerals
We wanted the cute Easter bunny hopping
　　around the lawn
We thought religion is good for the kiddies.

Now all of a sudden you've turned against us.
　　We wanted peace and you brought us a sword.
Things were going along all right.
　　then you got interested in the poor people
now they're strutting around like they are
　　going to inherit the earth.

Now all of a sudden you tell us to love our enemies.
Do you know what will happen if we do?
　　They will nail our hide to the wall and what
will we do then keep on praying for them?

We liked you when you were a little boy
　　gentle, meek and mild
cooing in your cradle
　　all those nice shepherds and angels
and we felt just awful about King Herod.

Look at all we did for you.
　　We made a national holiday in your honor.
We built big industries around it
　　Christmas cards, toy machine-guns for
the kiddies all those fancy gift-wrapped
　　whiskey bottles.

We built pretty churches in your honor
　　stained glass, organs, the works
and when the people moved away from the
　　riffraff

the church followed them
　　straight out into the suburbs.

Look at all we've done for you, Jesus
　　why can't you leave us alone?
We've got enough troubles now
　　why do you keep poking us in the conscience?
What do you want, our hearts? [2]

Closing Prayer

O Thou who art busy with every man, enable us,
by thy Spirit, to face up to more in Christmas
than we have ever understood before.

Help us to want what thou hast promised; to hear
what thou hast said; and to receive thy gift on
thy terms—to our salvation and thy glory.
Through Jesus Christ our Lord.

Amen.

CHAPTER 17

Jesus, Did You See Me Wave?

It isn't likely that the rock opera Jesus Christ Superstar *will* any time soon make the world forget Handel's *Messiah* or Stainer's *Crucifixion*. On the other hand, only the most introverted classicist would refuse to concede that Andrew Webber and Tom Rice have a warm way of making the passion narrative live. People like Mary Magdalene, Pontius Pilate, and Judas Iscariot, glimpsed from new and creative angles, seem as real as the folks we saw on the ten o'clock news last night.

The impetus for today's sermon came from a line in *Jesus Christ Superstar* that is sung by the crowd as Jesus rides into Jerusalem on Palm Sunday:

> Christ, you know I love you.
> Did you see I waved?
> I believe in you and God
> So tell me that I'm saved.[1]

Over the years that first Palm Sunday crowd has not fared well at the hands of Christians. It is usually depicted as a fickle mob, misguided in its messianic expectations, more intent on holidays than Holy Days, theologically shallow. Bible students are quick to point out that the reception that was accorded Jesus that day was remarkably like the welcome given Jehu when he ascended to the throne as Israel's avenger.

But doesn't that crowd deserve better at our hands? Those people did not have the benefit of two thousand years of hindsight. If they were confused about their "Coming One," what shall we say about the lack of clarity on eschatology in the Christian church today? Fickle? Maybe. Perhaps when all the facts are in, we will discover that many of the charter members of the mother church in Jerusalem had been part of the crowd that day.

What makes these people stand out as attractive and beautiful to me is the fact that they were sufficiently free to act on the impulse to rejoice in God. Parades have a way of stirring up the emotions and releasing us from our inhibitions. I shall remember for a long, long time that ride across 125th Street in the motorcade that bore the body of Whitney M. Young, Jr., to the airport. I can still see the faces that lined the way and pressed in close upon the slowly moving cars. There were smiles, waves, tears, and gestures of encouragement. There was pathos. Ramsey Clark told me a little later on in Kentucky that the most moving part of all to him was the sight of a little girl in her mother's arms who kept cupping and uncupping her hands. As Mr. Clark's car went by she whispered, "Mommie told me that I shouldn't wave." But even under those somber circumstances the heart felt the need to express itself, and she could do no other.

My question to us is this: who are we to sit in judgment on those first Palm Sunday enthusiasts? After all, their demonstration was marked by a rare self-forgetfulness. There was much running about. No one maintains his dignity while running except an athlete. Do you remember how you looked the last time you chased a subway train as its doors were rapidly closing? The waving of palm branches is not exactly prescribed behavior. They took off their garments and laid them on the donkey and then scattered them on the road. This is not something that they were practiced in doing. There was no hesitation about parting with their coats, no wondering, no debate as to whether there might be a cheaper way to show love and respect.

Giovanni Papini, in his still moving *Life of Christ,* describes their action this way: "The ass's back is hard, and Christ's friends throw their cloaks over it. Stony is the slope which leads from the Mount of Olives, and the triumphant crowds throw their mantles over the rough stones. This, too, is symbolical of self-consecration. To take off your mantle is the beginning of stripping yourself, the beginning of that bareness which is the desire for confession and the death of false shame; bareness of the body, promising naked truth for the soul. The loving charity of supreme alms-giving; to give what we have on our backs. 'If any man . . . shall take away thy coat, let him have thy cloak also.' " [2]

And here we sit on Palm Sunday, in our opulent respectability, looking in judgment on them because they dared to express their joy, we who, perhaps, have never once shouted a single "hurrah" for Jesus Christ. Halford Luccock said it with whimsy and point: "I was impressed several years ago that Eugene Ormandy dislocated a shoulder while leading the Philadelphia Orchestra. I do not know what they were playing. Certainly not Mozart. Perhaps Stravinsky. But at any rate, he was giving all of himself to it! And I have asked myself sadly, 'Did I ever dislocate anything, even a neck-tie?' " [3]

What is it that holds us back and keeps us so tightly wound

that our religion seems in the eyes of youth a somber and austere business? Have we sold our sense of wonder for security? Perhaps we've learned as we've grown older and richer that one gets along better in this world if he keeps his hosannas to himself.

Or does our mode of dress keep us from entering upon the glory that we see? For me the most interesting part of Charles Reich's book *The Greening of America* has to do with his analysis of the clothing of the young. He makes the point that when a businessman comes upon a patch of grass, let's say in the spring, and something of the little boy inside him says, "Why don't you sit and enjoy it?" he cannot do it, because he has his suit to consider. He doesn't wish to stain or tear it. His dress separates him from the earth and life's elemental pleasures. But along comes a youngster in dungarees, and he's ready for anything—to make a deposit in the bank, to sit down on the grass and enjoy the feel of God's good earth. We pay a price for our sartorial respectability!

Or can it be we really lack confidence in our ability to know the praiseworthy when we see it? Some people are afraid to say whether they enjoyed a book or not until they see what the key reviewers have written about it. They are not sure when they see a play whether it's a good one or a bad one for them until they see what the critics made of it.

We tend to be like a bevy of docile tourists on a guided trip. We like to have the world's attractions catalogued and starred for us so that we will know where to look. Did Moses when he saw the burning bush perhaps ask, "Is this one of the seven wonders of the Sinai Peninsula?" He turned aside to see, and he stayed to worship.

Or can it be that we have grown so dull to faith that mere "words about" have become a substitute for the real thing? Words as symbols of the real can keep us from experiencing the real.

It always brings a Christian up short to recall Kierkegaard's story of the geese sequestered in a yard. Every seventh day these geese paraded to a corner of the yard, and their most eloquent orator got up on the fence and spoke of the wonders of geese. He told of the exploits of the forefathers who dared to mount up on wings and fly all over the sky. He spoke of the mercy of the creator, who had given geese wings and the instinct to fly. This deeply impressed the geese who nodded their heads solemnly. All this they did. One thing they did not do. They did not fly, for the corn was good and the barnyard was secure.

> Christ, you know I love you.
> Did you see I waved?

Along with the spray of palm that you take home with you today I should like humbly to ask that you take home two lessons as well. The first is, *meet any glory that you happen on halfway*—wherever you meet it. Where you see glory passing by, bend with it, bend to it. We tend to stay underwhelmed because we refuse to allow ourselves to be overwhelmed by the magnitude of the love of God. Mistakes of the passion can be corrected but what can one do for inertia? Seize the moment, even if it makes you late or truant for something else. When Zacchaeus of Jericho heard that Jesus was coming to town, he shut down his tax office and climbed a tree, and that day changed his whole life. Remember that Martha was so intent on keeping the meal to schedule that she missed an unrepeatable chance to exult in her Lord.

William Cowper, the hymn writer, presents an angle of vision on this point that is unmatched in any other hymn I know.

> Sometimes a light surprises
> The Christian while he sings;

It is the Lord who rises
With healing in His wings:
When comforts are declining,
He grants the soul again
A season of clear shining,
To cheer it after rain.

Though vine nor fig tree neither
Their wonted fruit shall bear,
Though all the field should wither,
Nor flocks nor herds be there;
Yet the God the same abiding,
His praise shall tune my voice,
For while in Him confiding
I cannot but rejoice.[4]

The other lesson is this: *respect your encounters with God as the truest indication of your life.* The tendency is to be suspicious of our luminous, rapturous moments, to denigrate them, to see them as harmless interludes in an otherwise rational life. But the testimony of the saints is that we should disbelieve more often the strict logic of our life and trust ourselves more fully to our times of vision. This is when you are really you—when the fires of the eternal are consciously present in your life.

Our language works to deceive us here. Look at the word *ecstasy,* for example, which literally means "to stand out of." When someone, perhaps like a member of the crowd on that first Palm Sunday, loses himself in rapturous joy, we say of him that he is ecstatic, that he is standing out from himself. But what if it actually be the case that when a man is sullenly rational he is out of himself, and only truly himself when he rejoices?

When we reflect on one of our own experiences of great joy, we say to a friend, half apologetically, "I was beside my-

self." No, you weren't. That was your truest self. Your coldly
logical, rational self is really the put-on.

Or again, reflecting on a rapturous moment, we often say,
"I don't know what happened to me. I got carried away." You
weren't carried away. You were carried back. Carried back
to what you were meant to be—a son of the living God
capable of communion with your Father in heaven. When
liberating times of exhilaration come, we should meet them
at least halfway and respect and revere them as the surest
indications of our life!

On Monday evening, November 23, 1654, a brilliant
French physicist and philosopher was reading his Bible. Suddenly the whole room became illuminated. Blaise Pascal could
only think to describe this encounter with God in terms of
Fire, double exclamation point!! "God of Abraham, God of
Isaac, God of Jacob, not of philosophers and scholars. Certitude, certitude, feeling, joy, peace, God of Jesus Christ!"
Blaise Pascal wrote out two copies of this experience, one
on parchment and one on paper, and sewed them into the
lining of his coat so that he could remember the luminous
moment that transformed his life and shaped the balance of
his years.

> Christ, you know I love you.
> Did you see I waved?

A veteran student of business management has noted that
"when one first joins the ranks of management, he has zero
experience and 100 percent enthusiasm. By the time one dies
or retires, his mixture is 100 percent experience and zero
enthusiasm. In between these extremes, there is a relatively
short time in one's career when he has the optimum combination of both experience and enthusiasm." [5] That's what we're

looking for, isn't it? The optimum combination of experience and enthusiasm.

"Jesus, did you see me wave?" Perhaps we can hear him answer softly, "I've seen you study. I've seen you worship. I've seen you give. I've seen you serve. But I've never seen you wave. Is something holding you back?"

Closing Prayer

Lord, we covet the freedom to respond
    to thee with all our heart, soul,
    mind and strength.
Forgive us our caution,
    our acute self-consciousness,
    our fear of spontaneity,
    the hosannas that languish
      on our tongues
And make us the glad and contagiously
    radiant followers of the king
    that we were meant to be.
    Through Jesus Christ our Lord.
              Amen.

CHAPTER 18

The Man Who Left Too Soon

But Peter followed him at a distance, as far as the courtyard of the high priest, and going inside he sat with the guards to see the end.

Matthew 26:58, RSV

Only those who have nursed great expectations can know great disappointment. Only those who have tried hard to win can know the pangs of defeat. Only those who have dared to hope can know the meaning of despair.

That's why my heart goes out to Simon Peter—one of the most tragic figures connected with the Passion of our Lord. Peter had given it a good shot ever since that day when Jesus crossed his path and said, "Live for me." Slowly but surely, Jesus' kingdom talk was getting through to him. Rough and burly type that he was, he had grown to appreciate those frail intangibles—faith, hope, and love.

But after Palm Sunday things had started to slip. Jesus' opponents began to compose their ranks against him. Jesus, for his part, ruffled a few feathers by throwing the money-changers out of the temple and cursing the fig tree. After

that memorable Thursday supper, Peter had tried in the
garden to help the cause by the swift use of his sword. But
all he got for his trouble was a reprimand from Jesus.

Then came in swift succession the traitor's kiss, the instant
arrest, and the trial before the high priest Caiaphas. The big
fisherman saw the handwriting on the wall. The record tells
us that "he followed Jesus at a distance as far as the courtyard
of the high priest, and going inside he sat with the guards to
see the end." It was the end not only of Jesus' life, but of all
that Jesus represented, stood for, and embodied. The curtain
was coming down with a thud. "He went inside and sat with
the guards to see the end."

Millions in our world today sit where Peter sat that night
—to see the end. Disillusionment blankets many and many
a heart. The feeling persists that some grim inevitability is
moving in upon us. That it's just a matter of time. And so
we sit to watch the end.

Sitting is the appropriate posture, for there is nothing
more that we can do. We sit to watch the end. The end of the
United Nations; the end of Western civilization; the end of
law and order; the end of credibility in government; the end
of the civil rights movement; the end of the family as we
have known it; the end of religion; the end of the church.
Yes, even the end of God!

It is a heavy business trying to go on living as those upon
whom the ends of the world are come. This is why a new
isolationism is building in this country, at both the public
and personal levels, a decided retreat from history, a feeling
of "what's the use?"

Many young people in the current so-called Jesus movement are burned-out activists who found that they couldn't
change the world in two summer vacations. And so they
have retreated into the womb of an ahistorical piety. What
difference does anyone's effort make? Trying to help history

along is about as futile as rearranging the deck chairs on the *Titanic!*

A new hedonism can also be detected among us. Let's take the pleasures of the moment, for there is no tomorrow. As the gospel according to Schlitz has it, "Grab all the gusto you can, you only go around once." And so we live in an endless ambience of fun and boredom.

If nothing matters ultimately, it is hard to see how anything, even personal pleasure, can matter presently. Perhaps we believe that if we plunge into enough pleasurable activities what's wrong out there will somehow go away. Maybe it is only a fiction after all. The cartoon depicted a motorist halfway underneath his station wagon, which had obviously developed a flat tire. It was a warm, broiling sun under which he worked. His children were peering out the rear seat window and offering their father advice. The tag line has the exasperated father responding to his children: "But we can't switch channels. This isn't television, this is real."

Most of us just rough it out, glad for the routine that keeps us occupied. We try, with a straight face, to make ultimate concerns out of attempts to curb inflation, the next election, the latest public scandal, the next vacation, the next raise. We are even willing to allow ourselves to become absorbed in the "non-problem problems" of Madison Avenue as they reach us by way of television: ring around the collar, spotted glassware, deodorants that lose their power after five o'clock, and the single razor blade that doesn't quite catch all the whiskers the first time over.

The truth of the matter is that when your life and mine are void of the transcendent they sink into the absurd. Without God we resemble nothing more than Samuel Beckett's two sad tramps waiting under that wilted tree for their lives to begin.

"Peter followed him at a distance, as far as the courtyard

of the high priest, and going inside he sat with the guards to see the end." Soon he would deny his Lord, which is to say, he would renounce his vision, and walk away from it all!

The good news of Easter is that Peter left too soon! The world was not coming to a stop—it was coming to a start! God reversed the sentence that man had imposed on Jesus. "On the third day he shall rise again" (Matt. 20:19b). Those who had come to Joseph's garden prepared to mourn left to rejoice. They had come walking, but they left running. "He is not here. He is risen as he said" (Matt. 28:6).

Death had done its worst, and its worst was not enough. God had now pronounced his divine "Amen" on all that Jesus came to do and say and be. The kingdom of God had a future after all. The twilight through which Peter had passed was not the twilight of the night, but the twilight of the dawn.

The Easter event that we celebrate has profound meaning for every last one of us on at least two levels. At the personal level Easter means that death need have no power over us. "Death's flood has lost its chill since Jesus crossed the river." With even greater certainty than the Psalmist, we can affirm, "Yea, though I walk through the valley of the shadow of death, I will fear no evil" (Ps. 23:4a, RSV). We lay our dead to rest in the sure and certain hope of the resurrection to eternal life through Jesus Christ our Lord.

But the Easter event also says something about the meaning of history. We dare not so privatize Easter that it has to do only with individual men and women and the life to come. Easter says a lot about history—personal, national, and global.

The Resurrection affirms God's intention to establish his kingdom here on earth. God's aim is not to evacuate the faithful but to work through men and women who share the

Galilean vision to bring the kingdoms of this world beneath the rule of God. "But after I am raised again, I will go on before you into Galilee" (Matt. 26:32, NEB). He still has business on this earth.

This does not mean that every human alignment now standing will stand; that current balances of power will prevail; that the institutions to which we are accustomed will survive unchanged; that familiar forms and structures—even of the church—will continue as we have known them. But it does most assuredly mean that God's purposes for men will ultimately prevail; that service will triumph over exploitation; that generosity will triumph over greed; that freedom will triumph over bondage; that grace will triumph over sin; and that love will be victorious over hate.

To live by faith is to believe that this is so. Against Auschwitz and Hiroshima, against Belfast and Bangladesh, against Vietnam and South Africa, against assassinations in Memphis and Dallas and Los Angeles—yes, and against the petty hatreds and antagonisms of your heart and mine—God sets the resurrection of his Christ and invites our trust. As one who trusted, Nicolas Berdyaev could say: "It is not possible for my faith to be shaken by man, however low he may sink; for this faith is grounded not on what man thinks about man, but on what God thinks about him." [1]

In the light of the Easter triumph we keep busy with our father's business here on earth. As Paul said, "We are afflicted in every way, but not crushed; perplexed, but not driven to despair; persecuted, but not forsaken; struck down, but not destroyed" (2 Cor. 4:8–9, RSV).

One day turned it all around for Simon Peter. Easter is God's "nevertheless" flung into the face of all that would assert itself against his will. Well may the trumpets sound! Well may our hearts be glad! God has won.

Peter left too soon. To think—to think that he might have gone the way of Judas and missed that day! One day brought him back. That one day can do as much for us.

One of my favorite poems is "Columbus" by James Russell Lowell. The poet in those lines feels his way into what it must have been like to have had Columbus' vision and to have faced the obstacles, first on land and then on sea, that the explorer had to endure. Towards the end of that poem the crew puts the pressure on Columbus to go back. All those days at sea and no sign of land. Food supply, water supply diminishing. They beseech him, almost to the point of mutiny, to turn back and head for home.

But Columbus begs for one more day. He cries out:

> "God, let me not in their dull ooze be stranded;
> . . . .
> One poor day!—
> Remember whose and not how short it is!
> It is God's day, it is Columbus's.
> A lavish day! One day, with life and heart,
> Is more than time enough to find a world." [2]

Closing Prayer

> Lord, bless thy word this Easter day
>   wherever it is preached and lived,
> to the end that it may be
>   accorded lodging in
>   the hearts of many
> to their eternal peace
>   and thine eternal praise,
>   Through the same Jesus Christ
>   our Lord who loved us and
>   gave himself for us.
>   Amen.

CHAPTER 19

Getting High on God

"Do not give way to drunkenness, . . . but let the Holy Spirit fill you."

Ephesians 5:18, NEB

This is a time of anguish and tribulation, a time of torment and unrest, a time of soul-racking pain and grievous national division. But it is also, thank God, the time of the Holy Spirit. We live after Kent State and the decision to invade Cambodia, after Augusta, Georgia, and Jackson, Mississippi, but we also live after the advent of God's Holy Spirit on the day of Pentecost! Can we afford to celebrate the Festival of Pentecost with the world so bent and bleeding? A better question would be: can we afford not to? We court disaster when we focus only on our problems and forget the sources of our power.

Christians have an unfortunate way of making too much or too little of the Holy Spirit. Sect-type churches in the Pentecostal tradition tend to overstress the Spirit. They play down the cerebral and encourage the emotional in religious experience, prefer spontaneity to order, demand inner holiness of life, and ecstatically acclaim the charismatic gifts.

But rather than sit in judgment on those zealous Christians, let us confess that conventional standard-brand church members are less aware of the Spirit, his gifts and power, than should be the case. It's as though we were afraid of the kindling power of the Spirit, as though we disdained enthusiasm of any kind. We know God as the Father over us. We know God as the Son for us and with us. But do we know God in us as the Holy Spirit?

St. Paul delivered a curious exhortation to the Ephesian church. "Do not give way to drunkenness, . . . but let the Holy Spirit fill you." This is a curious word, because the apostle dares to suggest that being filled with the Spirit is the Christian counterpart to being drunk. The King James Version has it, "And be not drunk with wine, wherein is excess; but be filled with the Spirit." And we may be sure that "wine" here is the real thing, not Welch's grape juice or Kool-aid.

This is not the only time that the Holy Spirit is associated with inebriation in the New Testament. On the day of Pentecost after people of diverse backgrounds had experienced the Spirit's renewal and empowerment, there were some at least who said, "These men are drunk." Peter wasn't altogether flattering in his defense of the crowd. He didn't say that drunkenness was beneath them, that they couldn't get drunk or wouldn't. He simply said as a matter of fact, "They are not drunk. It's only nine o'clock."

Mood alteration by drugs, soporifics, and alcohol is very common in our society. Those over thirty prefer to get high on alcohol. Some under thirty prefer to get high on pot or heroin or LSD. Perhaps if St. Paul were writing today he would say, "Don't get high on alcohol. Don't get high on drugs. Get high on God; be filled with the Holy Spirit."

What connection could there possibly be between the false elevation of excessive drinking and an experience of the Holy

Spirit? Well, for one thing, men drink for warmth and con-
viviality. Gordon Cosby, a good friend and the founding
pastor of the Church of the Savior in Washington, D.C., tells
of a time some twelve years ago when he was speaking as a
guest minister during Lent in a church in New England. The
service was particularly dull and uninspiring. The only things
that seemed to move were the collection plates. When the
service was over Gordon and his wife felt totally depressed at
the absence of life in that church. They drove for a while
before turning in for the night. The last room available to
them in a wayside inn happened to be directly above the
tavern. They didn't sleep much that night, but they were
impressed by the laughter, the sounds of happiness, the ca-
maraderie that came up from the floor beneath. Cosby was
moved to say, "I realized that there was more warmth and
fellowship in that tavern than there was in the church. If
Jesus of Nazareth had his choice he would probably have
come to the tavern rather than to the church we visited." [1]

All taverns aren't that cozy nor all churches that cold.
The point is that God intended that through the Holy Spirit
the church should provide for men and women the most satisfying and accepting fellowship anywhere under heaven. To
some degree the church is effective here. Remember that the
church operates without a committee to preselect members.
There is no screening to insure that likes join likes. We do not
gather in a church around anything as superficial as a hobby,
like stamp-collecting or flower-raising, or something neutral
like music. The church dares to say, "Whosoever will, may
come." Consider the opposites that the church enfolds: male
and female, rich and poor, liberal and conservative, pensive
and emotional, old and young, lettered and unlettered, black
and white, yellow and brown.

Joseph Haroutunian was keen to insist that Christians

should notice not only the Spirit working in them but among them, creating the kind of warmth and oneness that so many in our time apparently feel can only be achieved by drugs or alcohol.

Unfortunately for them, when the drugs or drinks wear off, there they are. I have had people who frequent the cocktail circuit tell me that the reason they drink is that they really couldn't stand each other apart from alcohol. And here we are in the church, standing each other, if you will, maintaining remarkably durable friendships despite the issues of city, nation, and world that threaten to undo us. However exasperated a member of this church might be because of the happenings of the day, he can always come within the bonds of this fellowship and say, "I belong." And this is of the Spirit.

Moreover, men turn to drink for joy. I am not a drinking man, but I confess that when it was my business to ride the train between Lancaster and New York City rather frequently, I always chose the club car when I could. I enjoyed the mirth, the laughter, the easy access of people to each other. Those who drink testify that alcohol relaxes their tensions, gives the world a rosier hue, and induces gladness in the heart. Unfortunately again, when the drink wears off the realities are still there. The problems do not vanish. And for every moment of exhilaration there comes a compensating moment of depression. At bottom, the glass is an escape.

In contrast, the fruit of the Holy Spirit in the believer's heart is abiding joy. God is here and in control. This knowledge comes by faith, and faith is engendered in the heart by the action of God's Holy Spirit. Feuerbach was prone to describe faith as the mere projection of man's inner hopes and ideals into the outer reality of a transhuman God. The only thing we can say to Feuerbach and others is that by the action of the Holy Spirit in our hearts we know we are the children of God and joint heirs with Jesus Christ.

It is the ministry of God's Holy Spirit to confirm the truth of who Jesus was and what he came to do in the hearts of men. Oh, we sorrow with the sorrows of the world to be sure. We are caught up in its convulsions, its movements and its countermovements. But always with a sense of scale, for we believe that history, whatever it includes, is "that which happens," as Jürgen Moltman says, "between promise and fulfillment." Our joy does not rise from the equilibrium of the nations; therefore, when that equilibrium is threatened our joy does not recede. The ground may, as it does just now, shake beneath our feet, but always we can say with Moses, "The eternal God is our refuge and underneath are the everlasting arms" (Deut. 33:27).

One of the things we Christians ought to be about these days as we mobilize to express our social and political concerns is to seek ways to express the joy the world so much needs. It bothers me that the church is associated in the minds of men with gloominess and gravity. So many prayers that ministers give at public occasions convey a sense of travail and death. Surely it is possible for us to be seriously engaged in the issues of the day while at the same time testifying to the joy that resides inside.

I have kept for some time now a copy of a prayer that was offered by Father John J. Hever of St. Joseph's Church, Belmont, Massachusetts, at a public banquet in the city of Boston. I imagine that the gathered guests were bracing for the usual funereal tones, prepared to endure a few moments of somberness before going on to enjoy themselves. Father Hever must have surprised them when he prayed:

> Almighty God, our Father and our friend, we know that your memory of earthly banquet halls is pretty grim, ever since that first Christmas eve when an insolent fellow in a greasy apron at the only hotel in town slammed the door right in your mother's pleading face. Well, the mills of God grind

slowly, but they grind exceedingly fine, and here we are today, twenty centuries later, on a continent that the inn-keeper never knew existed, speaking a language he never heard, and our very first thought before we sit down to our banquet tables is to stand in reverence and salute your un-dying name.

We are especially happy to make this prayer, O Lord, and we hope you are to hear it, because this time we are not in church and not in trouble. As a rule when we speak to you, we are either kneeling against the background of a stained-glass window, or buckling on a life preserver. It is either the routine of religion or the rush call for help. But today it is gloriously different. Today we want you to bless our joy as we stand poised for a few hours of genial festivity. Bless us then, O Lord, and in thy goodness, grant that the food may be well flavored, the service smooth, and—if it isn't asking too much—the speeches short.[2]

The fruit of the spirit is joy.

Finally, men turn to drink for strength. They feel stronger after they have had a few. Bold enough to tell the mother-in-law to go home, courageous enough to go in and ask the boss for a raise, equipped for taking on the world. I believe we have seriously misunderstood and left unappropriated the ability of the Holy Spirit to enlarge the powers of those who believe. In Gordon Cosby's church there are rather steep re-quirements for membership, one of which is the reading of a considerable body of semi-difficult literature. I asked Gordon how he could possibly ask housemaids and charwomen to read the likes of James Pike and Emil Brunner. He said he believed that when Christians honestly seek to know, God expands their mental powers and gives them the capacity to under-stand. He has demonstrated this year after year in the mem-bership of that congregation.

Most of us who would rise to testify to unanswered prayer

would likely have to say that most of our prayers that have gone unanswered have been prayers for things. But is there one of us who has prayed unsuccessfully for the enlargement of patience, self-control, courage, poise, self-understanding? Wherever the Holy Spirit has taken possession of men, ordinary people have become capable of extraordinary achievement. I have listened to polished and well-educated ministers whose words were delivered flawlessly but whose message carried no conviction. And I have listened to others who stumbled through a poorly prepared sermon whose words carried the weight of the eternal because they were delivered in the enlarging and capacitating power of the Holy Spirit. We haven't begun to explore the possibilities here. Every once in awhile in the marketplace, in the bank, in the apartment building, in the church, one meets an individual who is living out this quality of life. What impresses us about them is that their deeds stick, their words carry, their influence counts and their life convinces.

Outsiders looking on at Pentecost when the Spirit came were staggered by the boldness of men who heretofore had been run-of-the-mine. In a darkening hour we should systematically and humbly ask that the gift of courage might be increased in us. I like the way Sean O'Casey puts it in *Red Roses For Me* when he has Ayamonn say: "I am not one to carry fear about with me as a priest carries the Host. Let the timid tiptoe through the way where the paler blossoms grow; my feet shall be where the redder roses grow, though they bear long thorns, sharp and piercing, thick among them!" [3]

"Be not drunk with wine, wherein is excess; but be filled with the Spirit." The times cry out for God-intoxicated men. Of course we feel outmatched. Who doesn't? You may recall that in the last act of *Tristan and Isolde* Wagner pits a lone harp against ten assorted woodwinds, the entire string section, four horns, two trumpets, three trombones and a tuba. We know how the harpist must feel when called upon to play against all that. But it is the business of God's Holy Spirit to make us able for the day. Because we live this side of Pentecost a Christian may stand and say in confidence, "I belong! I believe! I can!"

Closing Prayer

Spirit of the living God, and promised gift
of our savior Jesus Christ, we open
now our hearts to receive thee anew.
Enlarge our expectations, deepen our sense
of belonging, and renew our joy to the
end that we may shine as lights in a
darkened world and make it easier for
others to know that thou art love.
Through Jesus Christ our Lord we pray.
Amen.

CHAPTER 20

The Invincible Kingdom of God

Now great multitudes accompanied him; and he turned and said to them, "If any one comes to me and does not hate his own father and mother and wife and children and brothers and sisters, yes, and even his own life, he cannot be my disciple. Whoever does not bear his own cross and comes after me, cannot be my disciple. For which of you, desiring to build a tower, does not first sit down and count the cost, whether he has enough to complete it? Otherwise, when he has laid a foundation, and is not able to finish, all who see it begin to mock him, saying, 'This man began to build, and was not able to finish.' Or what king, going to encounter another king in war, will not sit down first and take counsel whether he is able with ten thousand to meet him who comes against him with twenty thousand? And if not, while the other is yet a great way off, he sends an embassy and asks terms of peace. So therefore, whoever of you does not renounce all that he has cannot be my disciple."

Luke 14:25–33, RSV

More years ago than I care to remember I had a monkey on my back in the form of a partly finished doctoral dissertation. The residence work was done but the writing wasn't. Seemingly, I could not finish the job and yet I could not walk away from it. At one point, I was tempted to put a match to all the gathered notes, thus to end the pressure once and for all. My wife, however, intervened and suggested that we dedicate one vacation to finishing up the job. So for thirty straight days we got up at six every morning to wrestle with the Hebrew of the Book of Amos. What a way to build up Brownie points!

One of the most insistent pressures of life is the pressure of unfinished business. We hardly embark upon a project before some nettling voice whispers annoyingly within, "Think you'll ever bring this off?" On every side we are exhorted to plan ahead. But how can we plan ahead when we do not know what a day may bring?

The two parables of Jesus which head this chapter speak to this very theme. First there was the tower begun but not completed. Chances are that this was to have been an elaborate farm building. But somewhere along the way the farmer had overextended himself. His dreams outran his bankroll. Perhaps his crops had failed. He got as far as the foundation and that was it! The foundation just sat there in the ground grinning up and mocking.

Then there was the king with war in his heart who discovered that he had only ten thousand men while the enemy had twenty thousand. Said Jesus in effect, "Would not a king in such a fix buy himself a white flag, stop talking like a hawk and begin sounding like a dove? Would he not start pressing diplomatically for peace?"

The meaning in both stories is terribly clear. The problem comes with the application of the point. The traditional view applies them to the Christian life. Jesus is here suggesting that a man ought to count the cost before he signs up. He is pronouncing a caveat against impulsive enlistment. He is hinting that there will be hardships to face and suffering to endure. Better not to begin than, having once begun, to fall back. You wouldn't like to be in the position of the farmer who started what he couldn't finish. You wouldn't be so foolish as to embark upon a war that you had no chance of winning. Woe to the man too ambitious for his resources!

I confess that this view has never satisfied me. This is why, even though I love the parables, I was in the ministry some eighteen years before I attempted to preach on these. Frankly, it just doesn't sound like Jesus to surround commitment with this kind of caution. Rather, I hear him say, "Sufficient unto the day is the evil thereof" (Matt. 6:34b, KJV). Or again, "Seek ye first the kingdom of God, and his righteousness; and all these things shall be added unto you" (Matt. 6:33, KJV). Or, "If any man would come after me, let him deny himself and take up his cross daily and follow me" (Luke 9:23, RSV).

Besides, how does any one of us know what his response to Christ will be ten, twenty, thirty years hence? What if some day, God forbid, you should be approached by a man with a drawn bayonet who would ask, "Do you or do you not forswear your allegiance to the Christ?" Who of us knows what his reply would be?

As one dips into the gospels he discovers Jesus everywhere encouraging spontaneous enlistment. He finds Matthew at the tax office and says, "Come, follow me" (Matt. 9:9). And the record says that Matthew rose up and followed, just like that! He finds Peter and Andrew washing their nets by the Sea of Galilee and says, "Come and I will make you fishers of men" (Matt. 4:19). And the record says they straightaway left their nets and followed him, just like that! He looks into the eyes of a man of power, rich and young, and says to him, "Sell what you have and give to the poor, . . . and come, follow me" (Mark 10:21, RSV). As though, just like that, this man could pass from darkness into light. He gazes into the starlit face of Nicodemus and says, "You must be born again" (John 3:7b). As though right then and there this Pharisee of hardened legal spirit could receive the Spirit of the living God.

I am willing to concede that these accounts are probably

condensed. It is likely that Matthew at least went home to tell his wife where he was going. Chances are that Peter and Andrew ran an ad in the *Jerusalem Times* to see what some of their fishing gear might bring. I am even willing to concede that in the halcyon days of his Galilean ministry Jesus might have raised the standard some in order to ward off "rice-Christians" and front-runners. But having said this, I still cannot see Jesus as one who flashed the amber light of caution. I think he would have subscribed to our folk wisdom that it is better to have loved and lost than never to have loved at all.

Fortunately, these parables can have a different application. Men like Joseph Parker, William Barclay, C. H. Hunzinger, Peter Jarvis, and others insist that in these ancient stories Jesus speaks not of man but of God. They were probably spoken as Jesus was en route to Jerusalem for the last time. The climate had shifted from one of popularity to one of threatened persecution. The shadow of a cross fell upon the way. For the comfort of his disciples Jesus is saying through these stories that God can do what he sets out to do. "Which man of you" is a Greek idiom that means "none of you." None of you would be so foolish as to start a building that you had no chance of finishing. None of you would be so foolish as to embark upon a war that you could not win. Well, neither would God! The kingdom can be resisted, but it cannot be overcome. God has the means to win and God means to win.

Jesus conceived of his life and ministry as belonging to a larger purpose that reached back beyond the beginnings of history and forward to the end of the age. This is why Jesus was never guilty of the ministry of flurry. He had about him what our teenagers might call a "holy cool." "My Father worketh hitherto, and I work" (John 5:17, KJV).

He moved along steadily in this confidence. He never had

to revise his strategy. He did not switch his major in his junior year. He took no steps that he had to retrace. He spoke no words that he had to retract. There was no wasted motion in his mission. He never prayed that he might know the will of God, but only for courage that he might do the will of God.

In this same spirit of commitment to a larger purpose, he was able to take opposition in stride, every inch a master of it all. This is what so confounded Pilate. "Speakest thou not unto me? knowest thou not that I have power to crucify thee, and have power to release thee?" (John 19:10, KJV). Calmly Jesus answered, "Thou couldest have no power *at all* against me, except it were given thee from above" (19:11). He even had the temerity to believe that when his earthly time was finished the cause would still go on. He looked into the faces of an unlikely group of half-committed men and women and was heard to say, "As the father has sent me, even so send I you" (John 20:21, RSV).

Even more incredible, he confronted them on another occasion and said, "Fear not, little flock; for it is your Father's good pleasure to give you the kingdom" (Luke 12:32, KJV). God had not vacated. God was not dead. God was not in history merely settling for a tie with evil. God means to win. There are no unfinished towers in the annals of the eternal. There are no unwon wars chargeable to God.

If we had just one ounce of this kind of confidence in God we would stop hanging crepe, biting our nails down to the skin line, and singing those mournful dirges. Our problem is that we are so preoccupied with our own concerns that we have lost sight of the Kingdom of God. We have taken what was meant to be a theocentric universe and made it into a homocentric universe. Is it any wonder that we scare so easily?

We are so intent upon our own petty miniventures that if

things are not going well there, we wonder where God is. Can I honestly believe that God is on the premises to insure my peace of mind, my pleasures, my satisfactions, my successing? Can we seriously maintain, despite what Scripture teaches, that God exists to serve us, to cure our neuroses, rid us of our complexes and prosper our undertakings? This perversion of faith is expressed in a winsome way for me in Dickens' *Dombey and Son:*

> . . . Dombey and Son, those three words conveyed the one idea of Mr. Dombey's life. The earth was made for Dombey and Son to trade in, and the sun and moon were made to give them light. Rivers and seas were formed to float their ships; rainbows gave them promise of fair weather; winds blew for or against their enterprise; stars and planets circled in their orbits to preserve inviolate a system of which they were the centre . . . A.D. had no concern with *anno Domini,* but stood for anno Dombey—and Son.[1]

When by some strong act of will we extricate ourselves from such a narcissistic point of view, we tend then to elevate, abstract, and absolutize some subplot in which we are busily engaged. We take Roman numeral III, capital C, arabic 4, small e for the whole theme. This is where we are pouring it on, and if God is not coming through there for us we question his existence and wonder what happened to the Kingdom.

What is the big idea of history anyway? Is it to Americanize the world? I think not. This is why I have never been able to be the kind of superpatriot the American Legion wants me to be. What is the big idea of history? Is it to democratize the earth? Democracy comes to us from Athens by way of Paris and Monticello. But that to which we are committed has even deeper roots and a wider hope than this. Is the big idea to westernize or to easternize the earth? Is the big idea black power or white power or green power? Is the big idea to take my own political slant and live and pray and work against the day when that particular view is enthroned in the whole of these United States? I think not. For this reason I've never been able to be a back-slapping Republican or a tub-thumping Democrat. I find that neither party has a basket big enough for all my eggs.

I dearly love the religious tradition into which I was born and in which I was raised. That church has been on the premises for some four hundred years now. But I am not at all sure that God is going to renew its lease. It may be that in his own good providential way he may ask that church and others to offer up their lives in the interest of a larger and more forceful unity.

We are called to something more than this, or any of these. We are called to nothing less than participation in "The Invincible Kingdom of God." This is what history is all about—God seeking to reconcile all things to himself in Jesus Christ, to reverse the sentence of the first Adam and to establish a new humanity after the likeness of the second Adam, Jesus Christ.

Unfortunately for our computer-oriented minds, the Kingdom of God is not spelled out in clarity stark enough to satisfy our curiosity. The Scriptures do not read like a time-table for an airline or a railroad. There are only hints and shadows that come through, for this Kingdom is beyond definition. John did the best he could on Patmos when he saw the old merging into the new and could only think to say, "The kingdom of the world has become the kingdom of our Lord and of his Christ" (Rev. 11:15b, RSV).

Yet, for all of its ambiguity, this Kingdom is clear enough for faith. There is one master clue and that clue is Jesus Christ himself. For Origen was right years ago when he called this kingdom *auto basilea,* a self-kingdom, for the kingdom is just like Jesus.

A few seasons ago, the San Diego Chargers of the American Football League soundly drubbed the Buffalo Bills. It was a stunning victory, for only a season earlier the Bills had done the same thing to the Chargers. Following the game the reporters surrounded the winning quarterback. "How come a year ago defeat, today victory?" The young quarterback, knowing where his next pay check was coming from, wisely said, "The coach gave us a good game plan, and we stayed with it all the way."

This is one way of seeing the exhortation and counsel of the New Testament. This is the game plan. Not enough has been disclosed to indulge our curiosity, but enough has been revealed to enlist our loyalty and obedience. For within the Kingdom we know through Jesus Christ we can be certain that it's better to reconcile than divide, that it's better to serve than dominate, better to forgive than avenge, better to be prayerful than anxious, better to be humble than proud, better to love than hate.

"Ah! But it won't work," you say, "not in this kind of world." Would you begin a tower that you could not finish? Would you begin a war that you stood no chance to win? Well, neither would God! We are worrying about the wrong thing. Let's not waste any more Kleenex on the Almighty. There are many things God asks of us in Scripture. He asks our loyalty, our love, our prayers, our trust. He asks our obedience and our faithfulness. But there is no place in either the Old or New Testament where God asks our pity! He can bring it off! He has no unfinished towers, no unwon wars.

On that dark day which by an amazing transformation of language we have come to call Good Friday, our Lord made his way to Calvary. Some women, you will remember, broke out from the sides weeping for him. But Jesus rebuked their tears and said, "Women of Jerusalem, weep not for me, weep rather for yourselves" (Luke 23:28). The Kingdom had been in their midst and they had missed it.

William Claire Menninger, a devoted Christian and a brilliant psychiatrist, toured this country for years as lecturer and consultant. He was frequently asked the secret of a good and happy life. Menninger's answer was usually the same, "Find a mission in life and take it seriously." This, in part, is the good news of the gospel, that people the likes of us are invited to lose ourselves in the Kingdom that cannot fail.

Closing Prayer

Lord, pry us loose from those lost or
marginal causes to which we give
ourselves so freely, that we may
give ourselves to thy purposes
which cannot fail.
Counter our desire for wealth or
reputation with the passionate
urge to serve
after the manner of our Savior
Jesus Christ
in whose name and for whose
kingdom we pray.
Amen.

Notes

CHAPTER 1

1. Kurt Vonnegut, Jr., *God Bless You, Mr. Rosewater* (New York: Dell, 1965), p. 34.
2. W. Somerset Maugham, *The Moon and Sixpence* (Baltimore: Penguin Modern Classic), pp. 53–54.
3. Joseph Haroutunian, *God With Us* (Philadelphia: Westminster, 1965), p. 29.

CHAPTER 2

1. Hans Sachs, *Masks of Love and Life* (Cambridge, Mass.: Science-Art Publishers, 1948), p. 54.
2. R. E. C. Brown, *Dictionary of Ethics,* ed. John Macquarrie (Philadelphia: Westminster, 1967), p. 295.
3. Samuel Johnson, lines added to Oliver Goldsmith's *The Traveller and the Deserted Village* (New York: Cambridge University Press).
4. James Thurber, *The Years with Ross* (New York: Signet Books, 1957), p. 274.
5. Will Durant, *The Story of Philosophy* (New York: Garden City Publishers, 1938), pp. 358–59.
6. Maltbie D. Babcock, *Thoughts for Every-Day Living* (New York: Charles Scribner's Sons, 1901), p. 7.
7. Sachs, p. 61.
8. Nathaniel Hawthorne, *The House of Seven Gables* (New York: Washington Square Press, 1940), p. 191.

9. William Temple, *Readings in St. John's Gospel* (London: Macmillan & Co., 1961), p. 223.

CHAPTER 3

1. William Glasser, *Reality Therapy* (New York: Harper & Row, 1965), p. 50.
2. T. W. Manson, *Ethics and the Gospel* (London: SCM Press, 1960), pp. 67–68.
3. *New York Times,* 24 September 1970, p. 2.

CHAPTER 4

1. Edmond Cahn, *The Moral Decision* (Bloomington: Indiana University Press, 1966), p. 17.
2. Theodore Reik, *New York Times,* 1 January 1970.
3. George Santayana, *Persons and Places* (New York: Charles Scribner's Sons, 1944), p. 17.
4. James Reid, "The Purpose of Prayer," *British Weekly,* 13 March 1958, p. 4. Reprinted with permission of *British Weekly.*
5. A. E. Taylor, *The Faith of a Moralist* (London: Macmillan & Co., 1930), p. 108.
6. Reprinted with permission of Macmillan Publishing Co., from *The Everlasting Mercy* by John Masefield, p. 105. Copyright 1912 by Macmillan Publishing Co., Inc., renewed 1940 by John Masefield.
7. John Calvin, *Commentary on the Epistles to the Philippians, Colossians, and Thessalonians* (Grand Rapids, Mich.: Wm. B. Eerdmans, 1957), pp. 77–78.

CHAPTER 5

1. T. S. Eliot, from "Burnt Norton," one of *Four Quartets,* in *Collected Poems, 1909–1962* (New York: Harcourt, Brace & World, Inc., 1963), p. 175. Used by permission of Harcourt Brace Jovanovich, Inc., publishers.
2. *Random House Dictionary of the English Language,* unabridged, 1967.

3. "Letters to the World's Editors," *Saturday Review,* 9 December 1967, p. 51.
4. Hugh Thompson Kerr, *Mystery and Meaning in the Christian Faith* (Toronto: Ryerson Press, 1958).
5. Lesslie Newbigin, *Honest Religion for Secular Man* (London: SCM Press, 1966), p. 31.
6. Nicolas Berdyaev, *The Beginning and the End* (New York: Harpers), p. 141.
7. William Cowper, "God Moves in a Mysterious Way," in *Pilgrim Hymnal* (Boston: Pilgrim Press, 1958), no. 87.
8. Nathan M. Pusey, *The Age of the Scholar* (Cambridge, Mass.: Harvard University Press, 1965), p. 145.

CHAPTER 6

1. Ben Arabi, quoted by Yves M. J. Congar in preface of *That Man Is You* by Louis Evely, trans. Edmond Bonin (Westminster, Md.: Newman Press, Deus Book, 1964).
2. Wolfhart Pannenberg, *Theology and the Kingdom of God* (Philadelphia: Westminster, 1969), p. 87.
3. Hendrikus Berkhof, *Christ, the Meaning of History* (Richmond: John Knox Press, 1966), p. 191.

CHAPTER 7

1. John Finley, *The Mystery of the Mind's Desire* (New York: Macmillan, 1936), p. 36.
2. From *For Days and Days* by Annette Wynne. Copyright 1919 by J. B. Lippincott Company. Copyright renewed 1947 by Annette Wynne. Reprinted by permission of J. B. Lippincott Company.
3. Joseph Haroutunian, *God With Us* (Philadelphia: Westminster, 1965), p. 25.
4. Harry Kemp, "Blind" in *Great Poems of the English Language,* comp. Wallace Briggs (New York: Tudor Publishing Co., 1936), p. 1294.
5. Michael Novak, *Belief and Unbelief* (New York: Mentor-Omega Books, 1965), p. 11.

6. Graham Greene, *The Power and the Glory* (New York: Viking Press), p. 29.
7. Walter L. Lingle, *Presbyterians, Their History and Belief* (Richmond: John Knox Press, 1944), p. 63.
8. P. T. Forsyth, *Positive Preaching and the Modern Mind* (London: Independent Press, 1907), p. 18.
9. Malcolm Muggeridge, *Jesus Rediscovered* (Garden City, New York: Doubleday, 1969), p. 4.
10. Ibid., pp. 7–8.
11. Hugh Thompson Kerr, *A Compend of Luther's Theology* (Philadelphia: Westminster), p. 56.
12. George Bernard Shaw, *Saint Joan,* act 1, sc. 5 (New York: Modern Library, 1924), p. 118.

CHAPTER 8

1. John Gassner, *Best American Plays, 1952–57,* 4th ser. (New York: Crown Publishers), p. 428.
2. Stephen C. Rose, *The Grass Roots Church* (Nashville: Abingdon, 1966), p. ix.
3. George A. Buttrick, *God, Pain, and Evil* (Nashville: Abingdon, 1966), p. 72.
4. Aristophanes, *The Frogs,* trans. Richard Lattimore (Ann Arbor: University of Michigan Press, 1962), p. 86.
5. Rollo May, *Love and Will* (New York: W. W. Norton, 1969), p. 270.

CHAPTER 9

1. Recounted by James I. McCord in "Perspective on Man," in *The Princeton Seminary Bulletin* 62, no. 1 (Winter 1969): 16.
2. Plato, *Republic,* trans. B. Jowett (New York: Walter J. Black, 1942), bk. 4, p. 314.
3. George Jackson, *The Prison Letters of George Jackson* (New York: Bantam Books, 1970), p. 135.
4. Quoted in Paul Tillich, *Love, Power and Justice* (New York: Oxford University Press, Galaxy Books, 1960), p. 67.
5. *New York Times,* 30 January 1972.

6. Ramsey Clark, *Crime in America* (New York: Simon & Schuster, Pocket Books, 1971), p. 192.

CHAPTER 10

1. A. C. Spectorsky, *The Exurbanites* (Philadelphia: J. B. Lippincott, 1955), p. 119.
2. Pope Paul VI, "On the Development of Peoples" from the papal encyclical *Populorum Progressio*, United States Catholic Conference, 26 March 1967.
3. J. Irwin Miller, "The Revolutionary Role of Business," *Saturday Review*, 13 January 1968, p. 68.

CHAPTER 11

1. George Buttrick, *God, Pain, and Evil* (Nashville: Abingdon, 1966), p. 43.
2. Gerhard von Rad, *Genesis* (Philadelphia: Westminster, 1961), p. 58.
3. Jerome Kretchmer, *New York Times,* 1 September 1970.
4. Henry David Thoreau, "On Being Busy."
5. Peter A. Jordan, *A New Ethic for a New Earth,* ed. Glenn C. Stone (New York: Friendship Press, Faith-Man-Nature Group, 1971), pp. 95–96.

CHAPTER 13

1. Lesslie Newbigin, *Honest Religion for Secular Man* (London: SCM Press, 1966), p. 129.
2. Leopold Tyrmand, "Reflections—Revolution and Related Matters," *The New Yorker,* 16 August 1969, p. 42.
3. Leonard Woolf, *The Journey Not the Arrival Matters: An Autobiography of the Years 1939–1969* (New York: Harcourt, Brace & World), p. 217.
4. T. C. Vriezen, *An Outline of Old Testament Theology* (Boston: Charles T. Branford Co., 1958), p. 371.
5. W. H. Auden, "For the Time Being: A Christmas Oratorio." Copyright 1944 and renewed 1972 by W. H. Auden. Re-

printed from *Collected Longer Poems,* by W. H. Auden, by permission of Random House, Inc.

CHAPTER 14

1. Jacques Ellul, *Violence* (New York: Seabury Press, 1969), p. 119.
2. Ibid., p. 69.
3. Patrick K. Kirby, *"Song for These Days,"* in *The Christ of the Poets* by Edwin Mims (Nashville: Abingdon, 1949), p. 241.

CHAPTER 15

1. Carlyle Marney, *The Recovery of the Person* (Nashville, Abingdon, 1963), p. 107.
2. Gerhard Ebeling, "Word and Faith," *The Expository Times,* December 1963, p. 76.
3. Albert Lasker, *Saturday Review,* 3 March 1956, p. 5.
4. Robert Browning, "Shop," in *The Complete Poetic and Dramatic Works of Robert Browning* (Cambridge, 1895), p. 810.
5. D. H. Lawrence, "Mystic."
6. Marilyn Plowman, "Ultimate Concern," *Christian Century,* 13 November 1963.
7. W. H. Auden, "For the Time Being: A Christmas Oratorio." Copyright 1944 and renewed 1972 by W. H. Auden. Reprinted from *Collected Longer Poems,* by W. H. Auden, by permission of Random House, Inc.

CHAPTER 16

1. J. D. Salinger, *The Catcher in the Rye* (New York: Signet Books, 1945), p. 125.
2. Andrew Blackwood, Jr., "Jesus, What Have You Done to Us?" *Presbyterian Life,* 15 January 1969. Copyright *Presbyterian Life.* Used by permission.

CHAPTER 17

1. "Simon Zealotes," from the rock opera *Jesus Christ Super-*

star. Lyrics by Tim Rice. Music by Andrew Lloyd Webber. © Copyright 1970 by Leeds Music Limited, London, England. Sole Selling Agent, Leeds Music Corporation, 445 Park Avenue, New York, N.Y. 10022. Used by permission. All rights reserved..

2. Giovanni Papini, *Life of Christ,* trans. Dorothy Canfield Fisher (New York: Harcourt, Brace & Co., 1923), p. 245.
3. Halford Luccock, *Communicating the Gospel* (New York: Harper, 1954), p. 145.
4. William Cowper, "Trust and Confidence," 1779.
5. Saul M. Silverstein, *"C'est La Vie,"* *PHP,* October 1970, p. 9.

Chapter 18

1. Nicolas Berdyaev, *Dream and Reality* (New York: Macmillan, 1951), p. 180.
2. James Russell Lowell, *The Complete Works of James Russell Lowell* (Boston: Houghton Mifflin; Riverside Press, 1896), p. 59.

Chapter 19

1. Elizabeth O'Connor, *Call to Commitment* (New York: Harper & Row, 1963), p. 109.
2. Copyright 1962 by *Saturday Review* Co. First appeared in *Saturday Review* December 1962. Used with permission of *Saturday Review* and Father John J. Hever.
3. Sean O'Casey, *Red Roses for Me* (New York: Dell, 1956), act 1, pp. 274–75.

Chapter 20

1. Charles Dickens, *Dombey and Son* (New York: Dodd, Mead & Co., 1950), p. 2.